Psychoanalysis as Biological Science

Psychoanalysis as Biological Science

A Comprehensive Theory

John E. Gedo, M.D.

The Johns Hopkins University Press
Baltimore and London

© 2005 The Johns Hopkins University Press
All rights reserved. Published 2005
Printed in the United States of America on acid-free paper
9 8 7 6 5 4 3 2 1

The Johns Hopkins University Press
2715 North Charles Street
Baltimore, Maryland 21218-4363
www.press.jhu.edu

Library of Congress Cataloging-in-Publication Data

Gedo, John E.
    Psychoanalysis as biological science : a comprehensive
theory / John E. Gedo.
        p.   cm.
    Includes bibliographical references and index.
    ISBN 0-8018-8051-3 (hardcover : alk. paper)
    1. Psychoanalysis. 2. Biological psychiatry.
    [DNLM: 1. Psychoanalytic Theory. 2. Biological Psychiatry.
3. Mental Disorders—psychology. 4. Mental Disorders—therapy.
5. Psychoanalytic Therapy—methods. WM 460 G296p 2005]
I. Title.
RC504.G3842 2005
616.89′17—dc22

                                            2004012072

A catalog record for this book is available from the British Library.

Contents

vi   *Contents*

Preface

Many psychoanalysts feel nostalgia for the heroic age of their discipline, when everything depended on the individuality and ingenuity of its pioneers. When one does not possess plausible hypotheses applicable to various contingencies in the clinical situation, one must fall back on artistic operations. Even today, our prevalent ignorance all too often compels us to resort to artfulness, and some among us do not feel the scientific obligation to develop coherent rationales for everything we do in analysis. Often, such attitudes are rationalized on the ground that psychoanalysis is a humanistic enterprise, embedded in art and philosophy. That is the romantic conception of the field.

There are respected contributors who actually prefer using metaphorical explanations even when operational concepts become available to replace them. Others deliberately choose to leave the aspects of analytic technique that constituted an art in an atheoretical limbo. Apparently, they take pleasure in obtaining good results by way of pure intuition—or the magical powers of a shaman.

For more than one hundred years, psychoanalysis has focused on human subjectivity and the uniqueness of every individual. To do so, it has had to concentrate on the world of symbols and their meanings, for most psychoanalytic data is collected by decoding the communications of analysands. At the same time, what differentiates psychoanalysis from other psychological systems is that these communications are processed in order not to study overt behavior but rather to focus on intrapsychic operations. This level of inquiry requires simultaneous use of biological and hermeneutic viewpoints, for whatever is unconscious necessarily lies beyond subjectivity.

A psychobiological viewpoint in psychoanalysis can only be based on the latest scientific views in cognate disciplines—brain science, cognitive psychology, semiotics. Hypotheses based on borrowings from these nonanalytic disciplines have been called "metapsychological." Freud, rightly named a "Biologist of the Mind," developed a set of these propositions early in his career;

three generations later, only some of his original ideas have proved to be valid. In recent years, abandonment of the metapsychology of 1900 has led many psychoanalysts (both the romantics among us and those who tend to look upon all theories with fear and loathing) to disavow the need to develop a valid biological framework for the field.

In this book, I hope to demonstrate the advantages of the view that psychoanalysis is a natural science and to outline a biologically tenable psychoanalytic theory of mental functions, their pathologies, and the techniques of treatment required to alter them. For, in the absence of knowledge, art comes to nothing—a warning first issued in 1400 to amateurs with ambitions to erect Gothic cathedrals. As I intend to outline a psychoanalytic theory, I shall concentrate on publications within that discipline, even when the biological issues involved transcend the boundaries of clinical psychoanalysis. Readers interested in the details of the biological research may find that information in references cited throughout the text. This book is, however, focused exclusively on the psychoanalytic relevance of the biological conclusions reached by cognate disciplines.

Part 1 is devoted to controversies about the very nature of psychoanalysis as a discipline: Can it aspire to scientific status? How much of Freud's oeuvre still qualifies as scientifically valid? What can replace those of his propositions that are no longer valid? Is it possible or desirable to construct a psychoanalytic theory without using biological presuppositions? What are the respective roles in psychoanalytic treatment of scientific observations and the interpretation of mental contents?

In chapter 1, I review the Freudian scientific contributions that have proved to have lasting value. In my judgment, the most important was the development of an entirely novel observational method through which Freud made possible the collection of reliable data about the inner life of human beings. The scientific hypotheses he formulated about these observations constituted the initial version of psychoanalysis. Many of these first thoughts have been revised in light of subsequent scientific findings about the operations of the central nervous system; yet initially even some propositions later refuted had heuristic value. Some Freudian concepts have retained their clinical relevance but need to be reformulated to detach them from untenable nineteenth-century biological premises.

Despite the passage of a century, several Freudian hypotheses have retained their scientific standing. Most important was Freud's realization that human thought is usually unconscious. Almost as essential has been his understanding of the import of the automatic repetition of basic patterns of behavior. That early childhood emotional vicissitudes play a role in structuring enduring mental dispositions was the psychoanalytic proposition that had the greatest effect in the social arena. Freud's distinction between two different modes of thinking also ranks among the most significant of his many contributions.

Despite the continuing validity of the foregoing propositions, Freud's metapsychological system, based on neurophysiological assumptions that were later refuted, is no longer tenable. This theoretical crisis within psychoanalysis came to light over a generation ago, at a time when no new biological framework to undergird its theories seemed available. Chapters 2 and 3 discuss the resultant turmoil in recent psychoanalytic discourse.

Some of the psychoanalysts who have lost confidence in Freud's metapsychology have, as a result, denied the necessity of dealing with the biological issues that set of hypotheses was designed to address. These theoreticians would confine the purview of psychoanalysis to mental contents; hence their orientation has been named *hermeneuticist*. Because the ultimate meanings of mental contents are difficult to determine, their interpretation must be "constructed" with the participation of the analysand. Yet analyst-patient consensus does not guarantee the reliability of their conclusions; in practice, the analyst's ideological commitment to one or another psychoanalytic school makes such reliance on hermeneutics alone excessively arbitrary.

By contrast, trained observers should be able to collect reliable psychobiological data; it is the accumulation of such data that actually constitutes the analytic knowledge at our disposal. This knowledge deals with functions such as cognition, affectivity, communication, and the regulation of behavior—matters Freud in his theoretical system encompassed via viewpoints he called economic and structural. An adequate theory of mental functions must take such matters into account. Without consensus about such a theory of mind, psychoanalysis becomes an arena of competing clinical hypotheses lacking in validation.

Many theoreticians deny any need for a metapsychology; they prefer to make psychoanalysis into "pure psychology." Yet none of these mentalists has succeeded in devising a theory that both covers the gamut of our observational data and refrains from introducing hidden biological assumptions. (Most contributors have disregarded the requirement of theoretical coherence as well.) Mentalists overlook the fact that clinical theories cannot be validated through data collected in the clinical situation, for most of the competing treatment algorithms yield similar results. Only evidence from cognate fields (all biological) can refute invalid propositions. The seeming effectiveness of widely differing interpretive schemata must mean that the actual therapeutic agent of psychoanalysis has not been identified but involves neither interpretation of mental contents nor the provision of a particular kind of relationship.

Changes in adaptation can only result from learning new skills, thereby altering the structure of the brain. These newly acquired functions may overcome apraxic deficits and make it possible to find better solutions for dyspraxic dispositions. Such biological alterations as increased affect tolerance, mastery of trauma, the ability to choose priorities, and better reality testing do not depend on the acquisition of "insight." Behavior regulation at the early phases of development (stages crucial for the acquisition of the biological vulnerabilities that constitute psychopathology) takes place on a biopsychological basis, without symbolic thinking.

The actual import of interpretation (and insight) in the clinical situation is outlined in chapter 4. Freud's clinical focus shifted from actual problems in coping with life to the realm of persisting mental contents when his therapeutic experience led to the realization that patients, in a seemingly paradoxical manner, resisted his efforts to assist them. They did this in ways that echoed their childhood transactions with caretakers. Freud called such treatment vicissitudes *transferences*. This essential clinical concept should, from an evolutionary/adaptive perspective, be understood as the biological capacity to classify current perceptions in terms of already meaningful categories. Whenever reliance on such established patterns becomes maladaptive, change cannot take place because its automaticity precludes the assimilation of novel experience. Only by means of accurate, timely, and tactful interpretation of the meanings of transference-resistance to learning does it become feasible to resume the acquisition of hitherto unavailable psychological skills. In other words, insight is an essential preliminary step in a curative process that must go "beyond interpretation."

In addition, the emergence of transference heightens the emotional intensity of psychoanalytic transactions in a manner that prepares the central nervous system to absorb what needs to be learned for better adaptation. Even the existence of the basic trust that makes cooperative treatment efforts possible constitutes the transference of early positive experiences with caretakers.

Part 2 shows that we now possess enough biological information to make it feasible adequately to address the principal questions about the regulation of behavior. Each of the major topics of a comprehensive theory of mind is separately discussed in ten successive chapters. Part 3 integrates these distinct issues into a single gestalt.

Chapter 5 is devoted to the question of psychological development and its pathological variants. It reviews the gamut of psychological disorders, primarily as derailments of the optimal development of the central nervous system and its dependent concomitants (affectivity, cognition, semiosis, and the regulation of behavior). Each phase of expectable development produces a specific type of psychopathology if its challenges are not adequately met. In addition, overall development may become arrested within any of these phases, thereby creating typical pathological syndromes. Such maturational failures predispose affected individuals to regression under stress and to emergency behaviors that are widely regarded as prima facie pathological. Seemingly maladaptive behaviors may actually be necessary to maintain self-organization and repair disruptions of that structure.

Self-organization should be understood to mean the individual's lasting hierarchy of motivations. Such a neural map of self-in-the-world is established before the acquisition of significant symbolic capacities. This means that the motivations involved are (almost) entirely those of the constitutionally determined human repertory that comes "on line" in a set sequence during infancy. The operation of these biological givens and the manner in which they are later amplified are discussed in chapter 6. In his metapsychology, Freud postulated that the forces that set the mind in motion are "drives." He classified these in various ways that attempted to encompass the expanding evidential basis of psychoanalysis. His ultimate differentiation of drives into Life and Death Instincts was not accepted by the majority of his successors. Recently, it has been postulated that biologically preprogrammed patterns of motivation operate on a cybernetic basis in response to specific stimuli. Complex human priorities are, however, not determined by such inborn patterns alone. With the increasing complexity of behavior regulation as the individual develops, the hierarchy of motivations is enlarged by those stemming from the formation of ideals and conscience. It is this hierarchy that constitutes the core of self-organization.

Acute disruption of self-organization is observable as the phenomenon of "trauma." In chapter 7, the significance of such actual or potential contingencies of mind/brain functioning is reviewed. Trauma was a neuropsychiatric concept Freud adopted to explain the biopsychological core of the pathogenesis of neurosis. Currently, there is consensus about its role in the production of various types of maladaptation, often in the form of automatic defensive efforts to prevent its recurrence.

Following the consolidation of self-organization, a sudden loss of organismic integration results in the fragmentation of the motivational hierarchy. This is subjectively experienced as confusion and/or some change in consciousness. In the era preceding the full achievement of self-organization, trauma is most likely to lead to the exclusion of the causative experience from consciousness—what Freud called *primary repression*. Childhood traumas that lead to such maladaptive avoidances have to be reexperienced and mastered in successful analytic treatment. Such mastery is contingent on using previously unavailable mental operations.

One of Freud's indispensable clinical concepts is that of defense. The principal defensive operations that generally constitute part of the adaptive repertory are discussed in chapter 8. These psychological mechanisms are put into operation to avoid the affective consequences of childhood crises, and they continue to operate automatically in adult life, although at excessive cost, for they preclude optimal information processing that would lead to more advantageous solutions of the matters at issue.

The importance of affectivity for adaptation is the subject of chapter 9; this basic ingredient of psychic life is a common biological property of mammalian organisms. Certain specific affects appear to be manifestations of patterns of functional change within the brain. As these phenomena come on line in infancy, they serve as essential communications from preverbal children to their caretakers. Subsequently, the latter ideally teach their children the meanings of the felt components of affectivity (i.e., a vocabulary of human emotions). Such symbolization establishes a system of signals from unconscious processes in the brain to consciousness; this attainment permits voluntary behavior that can reestablish affective equilibrium.

Affect recognition and affect tolerance are among the most important components of the adaptive repertory. The failure to recognize affects, *alexithymia*, must be treated by means of instructional measures. Lack of affect tolerance underlies neurotic pathology—the inability to resolve conflicts that leads to inhibitions or symptom formation. Mastery of anxiety states was at the core of Freud's understanding of "working through." Such mastery is not a cognitive achievement but a matter of retraining.

Chapter 10 is devoted to consideration of dreams and dreaming. Interpretation of dreams through the method devised by Freud was long considered a crucial therapeutic tool. Freud was mistaken, however, in postulating that the language of dreams is an archaic precursor of rational thought; it is currently understood as the natural language of the right cerebral hemisphere—a code different from consensual language. Dreams process the meanings of current experience in the light of the existing self-organization, the core of which consists of procedural memories preserved as affectomotor schemata. This is a neurological function common to mammalian organisms. Dream interpretation in treatment amounts to the correlation of primary and secondary processes, called *referential activity*. Patients differ markedly in their aptitude for apprehension of these equivalences.

Chapter 11 deals with behaviors observable in the psychoanalytic situation that directly reproduce modes of presymbolic functioning. The most prominent of these is nonverbal semiosis—motor enactments, paraverbal aspects of speech, or even automatic somatizations such as tics. In hypochondriasis, what is reproduced is a subjective sensation, mistaken for somatic pathology. Various alterations of consciousness constitute another category of archaic experience. Finally, early patterns of behavior may be automatically repeated so as to affirm the established self-organization—a process Freud called *repetition compulsion.*

Disorders of cognition are discussed in chapter 12. The most common forms encountered in psychoanalysis are magical thinking and obsessionality, which may occur together or separately. Delusions may temporarily appear as aspects of deep therapeutic regression in occasional analytic cases. A wide variety of more focal defects in cognition, such as lack of a sense of humor, inability to grasp the implications of human transactions, or mistrust of one's sense of reality, generally result from specific early childhood deprivations.

The next chapter takes up the controversy over the proper place of object relations in psychoanalytic theory. Relational theorists, misled by the inevitable prevalence of dyadic concerns in any treatment situation, overlook the centrality of the intrapsychic processing of all experience. Preverbal infants do not have memories of object relations; they only acquire affectomotor schemata. Inborn propensities for attachment promote the stability of the patterns of behavior learned in this process. Object relations are only one aspect of the more fundamental matter of self-organization.

Chapter 14 considers the precise roles of nature and nurture in producing permutations in sexual life. The specifics of what evokes sexual feeling are as yet poorly understood, although they are largely constitutionally determined. The outcome of the oedipal crisis decisively influences the choice of hetero-sexual versus homosexual objects, yet constitutional predispositions also play a role here. When the sexual system is recruited to subserve nonerotic ends, the resultant activity constitutes a perversion. The most frequent function of a resort to perversion is to counter narcissistic vulnerability, but fetishism appears to be a home remedy for impending traumatization.

In part 3, I propose comprehensive biological hypotheses about the regulation of behavior and psychoanalytic treatment. In chapter 15, behavior regulation is explicated in the context of a hierarchical model focused on progressive states of self-organization, correlated to those of the central nervous system. The subjective aspects of the motivational hierarchy consist of unconscious memories of affectomotor schemata. When consolidated, this leitmotif of identity must be maintained; it is, however, gradually modified through the repetition of novel experiences. The acquisition of symbolic functions and semantic memory permits the child to make judgments about its own performance and that of the caretakers; thereupon, issues of self-esteem take center stage in development, and a code of values should be accepted. Thereafter, primitive wishes give rise to intrapsychic conflict.

In adult life, derivatives of each of the foregoing phases of development are potentially available to facilitate adaptation. In stressful circumstances, regression to the more archaic adaptive modes may become temporarily advantageous. Personality disorders are conditions wherein archaicism permanently remains the prevalent state in all or part of the mental life.

Improvements in adaptation take place only as a result of new learning. Chapter 16 deals with what analysands need to learn in treatment and what has made them incapable of absorbing that knowledge in the course of day-to-day life—in other words, how such individuals acquire their learning disability. Theories of analytic technique have not dealt with the crucial problem of how such handicaps can be overcome. (We know somewhat more about what to avoid to make therapeutic success possible.)

In analysis, learning may take place through identification with the analyst's behavior, but such serendipitous changes are seldom sufficient. Analysands may have to be told about the deficiencies in their psychological armamentarium and assisted to overcome them through patient but explicit instruction. Because new neural networks have to be established, this is necessarily a slow process, complicated by the fact that it tends to be experienced as humiliating. Such work can only succeed if carried out in the context of positive transference.

Chapter 17 deals with the therapeutic process as it generally unfolds in a successful analysis. This has usually been described in terms of a succession of predominant transferences, without sufficient attention to the manner in which the analyst's technical choices are bound to skew these. It is more cogent to trace the shifts in the mode of hierarchical organization as these occur in reaction to analytic transactions. The maladaptive legacies of various phases of development are thus successively brought to light and potentially made available for remediation. Optimal tension regulation, unification of hitherto uncorrelated segments of the self-organization, the correction of illusions, and the capacity to live with conflict without disavowal or repression of either choice are the most significant improvements analysis may achieve. Analysis should take place in an ambience of empathy and safety that permits analysands to dare to show their true selves—currently unacceptable, archaic aspects of the self-organization.

The last chapter briefly lists some of the most significant problems, from a clinical perspective, that await solution through the emergence of novel biological findings. Most of these concern individual differences with regard to quantitative measures of characteristic behaviors in terms of qualities such as psychological strength, intensity, courage, and persistence.

I have appended a few "last words" about the current ambience of psychoanalysis, so unfavorable for the views I espouse. Most clinicians cannot even grasp what is meant by "psychoanalysis as a biological science." When I recently told a colleague that I was writing a book on that topic, he exclaimed, "Oh—you are interested in psychopharmacology?" No, that's not it . . .

Acknowledgments

This book would not have been written without the encouragement of Wendy Harris, medical editor of the Johns Hopkins University Press. She, in turn, had been introduced to my work by Professor Richard Perlman of the University of Chicago, editor of *Perspectives in Biology and Medicine.* They succeeded in overcoming the reluctance of an author who had recently published an essay "In Praise of Leisure."

The actual production of the book was made possible by the efficient assistance of copyeditor Julia Ridley Smith and the indispensable work of Eva Sandberg, who transformed my scribblings into computer disks usable by publishers.

Part I / Psychoanalysis as Science and the Role of Hermeneutics

CHAPTER ONE

The Enduring Scientific Contributions of Sigmund Freud

Psychoanalysis as a Natural Science

The new millenium happened to mark the centenary of the birth of psychoanalysis. Its sole parent, Sigmund Freud, has been dead for some sixty-five years—indeed, he was born before the American Civil War, relatively early in the reign of Queen Victoria—yet his contribution to modern civilization has been so profound that his work has stayed in the center of attention (whether to be praised or denigrated) throughout the twentieth century. The recent centenary of the emergence of this new discipline may constitute a suitable opportunity to reappraise Freud's complex oeuvre from a scientific perspective. His effect on Western civilization, however, was not primarily scientific—it consisted of the moral influence of his writings on the upbringing of children, on sexual attitudes, on views concerning personality problems, and so on.

One way to summarize his life's work is simply to state that he invented a new scientific discipline that has steadily grown for over a hundred years and in every part of the developed world—an intellectual and organizational feat of some magnitude. His scientific writings (in English translation) comprise twenty-four volumes (Freud 1886–1957) and continue to be read, not only by professional psychoanalysts. So great has been Freud's prestige in educated circles that, even today, two to four generations after its original publication, his oeuvre is commonly equated with the conceptual world of psychoanalysis, and fresh translations of his celebrated works are being prepared for the general public.

Recent discussions of Freud's work aimed at that general public have tended to focus on those of his hypotheses that have been invalidated by a variety of scientific advances. Because Freud unequivocally adhered to the conception of psychoanalysis as a branch of biological science, he attempted to correlate his observational data with the biology of his own time—specifically with the prevalent theories of contemporary neurophysiology. Brain science was in its infancy a hundred years ago, and the concepts Freud (1895a) borrowed from his neurological and physiological mentors—Wilhelm Brücke, Theodor Meynert, Josef Breuer—have not stood the test of time. In the most general sense, the functions of the central nervous system were then conceptualized in power engineering terms (as if the brain were an electrical apparatus), a paradigm that turned out to be incorrect (Toulmin 1978). Most of Freud's scientific errors followed from these invalid neurophysiological assumptions. (For detailed discussions of these complex issues, see Rosenblatt and Thickstun 1977, Holt 1989, Dorpat and Miller 1992, and Rubinstein 1997.)

It has taken psychoanalysis a half-century (and the presentation of valid neurophysiological information in psychoanalytic writings like those of Levin [1991, 2003] and Schore [1994]) to overcome the conceptual difficulties caused by Freud's mistaken assumptions. It is very odd that commentators who would not dream of dismissing current brain science because of the inadequacies of that discipline at the end of the nineteenth century often try to discredit contemporary psychoanalysis because it applied the very same hypotheses to mental life. Such critics appear to ignore one of the cardinal methodological principles of science, that progress in knowledge can best take place through the disproof of existing hypotheses. It is to Freud's credit that he generally stated his speculative propositions in such a manner that they could be invalidated by subsequent scientific findings.

Another way to put this point is to reemphasize that Freud placed his new discipline on *scientific* foundations—meaning that it did not spring from his head fully formed as a doctrine; rather, it was a first attempt to explain a broad array of novel observations, subject to continuous modification in the light of further experience. The *Standard Edition of the Complete Psychological Works of Sigmund Freud* still deserves careful study, for it contains important observational data and sophisticated thinking about them, but it is not a currently acceptable exposition of the valid knowledge that constitutes psychoanalysis.

Readers unfamiliar with contemporary psychoanalysis—the current consensus as well as the ongoing controversies within the field—may have difficulty evaluating which of Freud's propositions continue to have scientific validity, which have been invalidated although they attempted to answer important questions (and therefore possessed great heuristic value), and which of them turned out to be useless because the problems they were supposed to address were misconceived. In this respect, however, Freud's contributions are no different from those of other authors in the biological sciences who wrote sixty to a hundred years ago.

Development of the Analytic Observational Method

In my judgment, Freud's most lasting and valuable scientific contribution was not conceptual; hence it tends to be overlooked by nonspecialist historians. This achievement was the development of a novel observational method through which it became possible for the first time to gain reliable data about the inner life of human beings. From about 1890, when he began to practice the "talking cure" invented by Breuer, it took Freud roughly twenty years to standardize a psychoanalytic method that permitted independent observers to collect such data. These unprecedented observations about mental functions and the control of human behavior have defined the boundaries of psychoanalysis as a scientific domain. In other words, Freud accomplished a methodological breakthrough whereby he single-handedly founded a new discipline.

It is difficult to discern whether Freud fully realized that his method was no mere pragmatic tool to be used therapeutically. His most extensive exposition of the procedure was given in "Papers on Technique" (1911–1915), written shortly after he stopped modifying it. The context there was entirely pragmatic. Nor have subsequent commentators emphasized the *scientific* importance of Freud's observational method. I suspect that the clumsy attempts of some psychoanalysts to rebut critics by claiming that those who have not been in analysis have no way of assessing the truth value of psychoanalytic data were inadequate efforts to point out that the standard psychoanalytic situation permits the collection of information that is simply not observable in other settings.

A psychoanalytic situation requires periods of observation (analytic hours) almost every day—at any rate, as frequently as possible; in the course of these, the analysand must make good-faith efforts to free associate, while the analyst has to act as an empathic witness to the resulting productions as well as to the analysand's concomitant (nonverbal) behaviors. Free association differs from ordinary human discourse, which is almost always guided by social rules and the speaker's interest in preserving the privacy of much of his or her inner life. Its precondition of total candor, promoted by the reciprocal guarantee of complete discretion on the part of the analyst, tilts the associative process toward veracity, authenticity, and the emergence of mental contents most people prefer to keep out even of their own awareness. The resultant observations reveal aspects of mental functioning otherwise hidden from the view of the analysand, not to mention others.

Not only does the psychoanalytic situation yield data inaccessible to the nonanalytic observer; such data almost never become available through private introspection. This is true partly because we tend to view ourselves through the distorting lens of strong emotional bias and partly because hardly anyone is able to persevere with introspection in the face of intense shame, guilt, or anxiety. The presence of an empathic witness serves to challenge the analysand's prejudices and to push for perseverance despite emotional discomforts.

Because the manifold schools of psychoanalysis have disagreed about the significance of the data of observation they share, it has not been sufficiently recognized that they have few disagreements about the nature of those data. Albeit there seems to be widespread agreement that the analyst's therapeutic activities are bound to affect the subsequent emergence of fresh material, it has become fairly clear how particular interventions tilt the field of observation in specific directions. The simplest illustration of this tendency is that analysands generally focus their thoughts on matters that seem to interest the analyst (and to neglect those to which the analyst appears to be unresponsive). In other words, intersubjective factors influence the emergence of the observational data in particular settings, but this circumstance does not compromise the relevance of those observations for the analysand's mental life. In summary, Freud succeeded in devising a procedure that has led to the reliable collection of previously unobserved data about the human mental condition. Psychoanalysis is the science that has attempted to explain the significance of these novel observations.[1]

The Significance of the Unconscious

Only one of Freud's conclusions on the conceptual level can approach the scientific value of his methodological discovery—that is his realization that human mentation proceeds predominantly outside of subjective awareness (1900, chap. 7). Freud was not the first to record that unconscious mentation is possible; his great discovery was that conscious thinking (reflection) is the exception rather than the rule. By placing this insight at the center of his conceptual system, Freud differentiated the discipline he created from the science of conscious mental states; that is why psychoanalysis is also called *depth psychology*. By correctly discerning the topography of mental life, Freud went beyond the expansion of our understanding of the control of behavior—he made possible the improvement of that adaptive system by way of psychological intervention.

From this perspective, many psychological therapies that have rejected other Freudian propositions (such as the schools of the early secessionists from psychoanalysis, C. G. Jung and Alfred Adler) owe their genesis to Freud's discovery of the true significance of unconscious mentation. Homans (1979) and Stepansky (1983) have provided dispassionate histories of Freud's controversies with Jung and Adler respectively. It is important to note that Freud's hypothesis was a biological proposition that awaited validation through nonpsychological methods. Such proof became available with the development of positron emission tomography (PET)-scan techniques for the visualization of brain activity. These have amply demonstrated the validity of Freud's view on the relative significance of conscious and unconscious mental life (Lassen 1994). Thus psychoanalysis was built on the valid assumption that, in order to understand vital aspects of behavior, we have to discern the effects of what hitherto has been unconscious thought.

From such a "topographic" perspective, Freud (1926) reached another crucial conclusion: certain mental contents that had previously been conscious may arouse sufficient shame, guilt, or anxiety to set in motion a variety of mental processes that either render them entirely unconscious or deprive them of their emotional charge, disavow their significance, or shift responsibility for them to someone else. Arguably, Freud's description of these defensive operations—repression, disavowal, projection, and so on—may have gained wider public acceptance than any of his other scientific contributions. (Within psychoanalysis, they have been cogently summarized by Anna Freud [1936] and reevaluated by Gedo and Goldberg [1973].) In recent years, brain science has made sufficient progress to explain the neurophysiological basis of several of these defense mechanisms (Levin 1991).

The scientific importance of the conceptualization of a system of defenses against the experience of painful emotions is that it has illuminated both the adequate and the maladaptive organization of behavior. The failure of defense as well as the need to suppress vital aspects of one's true self through continual defensive operations constitute psychopathology, although of course there are many other types of maladaptation (Gedo 1988). Freud's insight about the frequency of conflicts between aspects of personal motivation and the need to avoid painful emotions has made it possible to intervene therapeutically (not only by means of analytic treatment proper but also through a variety of psychotherapies based on psychoanalytic principles) in a manner that may establish effective defenses without stifling the individual.

The Compulsion to Repeat

The third major Freudian achievement was the insight that human behavior is characterized by a variety of automatic repetitions. Freud observed that analysands were never aware of any motive for these behaviors, nor could an observer discover any in every instance; hence Freud (1920) rightly concluded that there has to be a fundamental biological basis, inherent in the organization of the central nervous system, for the tendency to repeat. The first type of repetition he discerned (1912) was that of patterns of behavior and attitudes initially experienced in relation to the primary caretakers of childhood. Freud observed that analysands reexperienced these patterns vis-à-vis the analyst— a process he named *transference.* He proposed (1914a) that transference repetition takes place in lieu of the recollection that might make it possible to transcend persisting childhood mental dispositions that lead to intrapsychic conflict.

From the clinical perspective, the conceptualization of transference made it feasible in most instances to transcend therapeutic difficulties caused by analysands' seemingly irrational emotional reactions to the analyst through interpretation of their significance as repetitions of aspects of the past (Freud 1915a). Transference interpretation is the therapeutic tool that has made it possible to conduct long-term analyses in the course of which the voice of reason may gain a hearing despite any initial distress caused by its message.

Freud (1920) eventually observed the obligatory occurrence of repetitive behaviors that produce neither pleasure nor profit; as he put it, these compulsive repetitions are "beyond the pleasure principle" that governs most unconsciously motivated activities. These were the instances for which Freud was never able to discover any motive; therefore he was forced to provide a purely biological explanation for them. His commitment to an energetic model of mental functions led him to the mistaken conclusion that the compulsion to repeat is caused by the operation of entropy (that is, the loss of organization). Because this hypothesis turned out to be unacceptable to most psychoanalysts, the important observations it was meant to explain were for some time neglected. In recent years, theoretical biology has emphasized the need to perpetuate the organization of complex living systems; this overriding biological principle (directly contrary to Freud's postulation of entropy to explain automatic repetitions) provides a rationale for the persistence of existing patterns, even if in current circumstances they violate the pleasure principle (Gedo 1988, 1993a; Modell, 1993). The mechanism of such persistence is now well understood in neurophysiological terms as the effects of repeated use on strengthening synapses. In other words, synaptic mechanisms, such as long-term potentiation, which are thought to underlie learning and memory favor repetitive behavior because whatever one has done is easier to do again (R. Perlman, personal communication, 2001). At any rate, Freud's twin discoveries of transference and the repetition compulsion turn out to be crucial components of adaptive behavior.

The "Genetic" and "Structural" Viewpoints

The last Freudian scientific discovery of major import (Freud 1900, 1909a, 1923, 1926) is the role of early childhood vicissitudes (the dire consequences of stressful experiences, illness and, above all, unfortunate family relationships) in personality development and pathogenesis. This concept is somewhat confusingly called the *genetic viewpoint* of psychoanalysis, although it refers to environmental vicissitudes, not to hereditary factors alone (Rapaport and Gill 1959). For the most part, Freud was able to reconstruct these pathogenic events only if they occurred during the era he labeled *oedipal*—roughly, between the ages of three or four and five or six; it remained for some of his successors to postulate the pathogenic consequences of even earlier vicissitudes (see Gedo 1986, 1999). The exceptions to this generalization demonstrate that his conception of a genetic point of view was, however, potentially broader than the period to which he applied it. For instance, he described the devastating effects of congenital abnormalities on character formation as a result of early injury to self-esteem (Freud 1916).

A close corollary of the conceptualization of a genetic viewpoint was Freud's (1918) realization that the long-term effects of early experience imply that it has left behind affect-laden memories that continue to act as structured mental dispositions, that is, enduring functional propensities. From this functional perspective, insight into the enduring effects of the (childhood) past constitutes the "structural viewpoint" of Freudian theory. It is the concurrent use of the motivational (dynamic), the topographic, the genetic, and the structural frames of reference that qualifies Freudian psychoanalysis as the most comprehensive attempt to characterize the regulation of human behavior (Rapaport and Gill 1959). Freud conceived all these metatheoretical viewpoints from a biological perspective, but that commitment is clearest in the case of the structural point of view because it refers not to the *contents* of mind but to the manner in which those contents are processed (1923). In other words, it was the structural viewpoint that provided Freud's psychological theory with its connection to neuroscience.

Freud tried to amplify that connection by postulating a complementary "economic viewpoint" that dealt with putative vicissitudes of psychic energy. His ultimate statement on this subject (Freud 1940) continued to maintain this concept. The hypothesis of psychic energy has become untenable as a result of more recent knowledge about the operations of the central nervous system.

Primary and Secondary Processes

Freud has rightly been dubbed a "biologist of the mind" (Sulloway 1979), for his important and lasting scientific contributions mentioned thus far (including the development of a novel observational method) can properly be characterized as valid biological discoveries. Paradoxically, his fame was not to be based on any of these contributions. The popular imagination was captured by Freud's reports of the conflictual mental contents he typically encountered in his clinical work. Because he was ever trying to find human universals, Freud's necessarily limited clinical experience was seldom sufficient to yield universally applicable conclusions about intrapsychic conflicts; thus most of his hermeneutic claims have subsequently proved to be of limited applicability. In other words, in the infinitely variable territory of mental contents, Freud's overly ambitious efforts to generalize turned out to be based on sampling errors.

Nonetheless, Freud (1900, chap. 7) made one universally important discovery about the contents of human thought, that of the distinction between the consensual language of adult discourse and the language of dreams, neurotic symptoms, parapraxes, and jokes (Freud 1900, 1901, 1905a; Breuer and Freud 1895). He designated these distinct languages as secondary and primary processes, respectively. Much of Freud's magnum opus, *The Interpretation of*

Dreams, describes in detail how the primary process operates and how it may be translated into rational discourse. Freud himself believed that his decipherment of the language of dreams was the greatest of his accomplishments. If there is no general agreement today about the appreciation of Freud's masterful clinical discovery, it is because he tried to fit his observations into the metapsychological (psychoeconomic) framework that has been invalidated, thus obscuring their significance. Moreover, it has been discovered that much of conscious thinking (particularly in creative endeavors) makes use of both primary and secondary processes (Noy 1969).

The Yield from Invalid First Thoughts

The foregoing list of Freud's lasting scientific contributions is by no means exhaustive, but from a contemporary perspective these are his observations and conclusions that continue to have the greatest value in explicating human behavior and its regulation. By contrast, a valid proposition such as Freud's (1905b) assertion that all human beings are bisexual has not, for the moment, found a prominent role in explaining these matters. Through the development of a novel observational method, Freud discovered a universe of fresh data that for the first time permitted proper appreciation of the role of childhood experience in structuring mental dispositions of crucial import for adult adaptation, gave rightful emphasis to the dominant role of unconscious mental processes as well as of primary process thinking, and highlighted the essential part played by the automatic repetition of old behavioral patterns in health and disease. These contributions alone would justify Freud's reputation as one of the foremost scientists of the past century.

The assessment of a scientist's stature should not, however, be based on the number and importance of valid hypotheses alone; it should include contributions to scientific progress through raising crucial questions and/or proposing hypotheses that may miss the mark but subsequently promote fruitful inquiry. Freud put forward too many heuristically useful ideas that are no longer regarded as entirely valid to allow me to discuss them all here; rather, I hope to convey the importance of such "first thoughts" about scientific puzzles by focusing on a few examples.

When the clinical experience of the early psychoanalytic circle began to broaden, it encountered character types who did not develop the kind of transference Freud had initially observed in his work with patients who only suffered from well-defined neurotic symptoms. This new finding confronted Freud with the inadequacy of his theory of motivation based on the concept of instinctual drives. He was not ready to scrap that theory because of a single "anomaly"; instead, he amended it (Freud 1914b) by postulating another form of drive, that of "narcissism." (Later investigators were able to discern specific transferences displayed by "narcissistic" personalities [see Kohut 1971], thus substantiating that through this concept Freud had come to grips with a real psychological entity.) In contemporary psychoanalysis, narcissism is no longer understood as the product of an instinctual drive (Gedo 1993a)—in other words, Freud's initial contribution on the subject was largely invalid. Yet the notion of narcissism was of such heuristic value that it has truly suffused modern views of humanity, and all students of human behavior have had to tackle the behavioral correlates of narcissism: selfish ruthlessness, arrogance, vanity, and ingratitude. Thus the conceptualization of narcissism turned out to be one of Freud's most fruitful scientific notions.

The Freudian concept of psychic trauma has had a similar fate. Originally, the idea was borrowed from neuropathology (Breuer and Freud 1895); when Freud gave up basing his work on the brain science of the 1890s, he retained the notion without specifying the physiological mechanisms it involves. Clinical observation has amply confirmed the reality of traumatic states—psychoanalysts encountered them in pure culture, so to speak, in numerous casualties during both world wars (Abraham et al. 1919). There is no controversy about the observation that psychological traumas suffered in early childhood may lead to maladaptive consequences. Late in his career, however, Freud (1926) offered an explanation of trauma on an untenable psychoeconomic basis that has now been abandoned by most psychoanalysts. Despite this invalid hypothesis, recent views of psychopathology (e.g., Modell 1993) have frequently been centered on the concept of trauma (now understood as the disorganization of established structure), so that this early Freudian idea has proved to have led to illuminating theoretical progress.

I shall have to content myself with offering only one additional example of a partially misconceived notion that led to fruitful results. Clinical experience led Freud to the realization (Freud 1914a) that correct interpretation of the analysand's mental contents did not by itself produce behavioral change. He postulated that, beyond interpretation, a process of "working through" is needed in order to master the affects previously warded off by defensive operations. There is universal agreement about the necessity of working through to achieve therapeutic success. It is not widely understood, however, that such a process is not merely a matter of mastering the unpleasure of facing the truth: behavioral change is contingent on the establishment of new neural networks (through novel activity patterns), thus disestablishing automatic reliance on those previously available (Gedo 1996, chap. 13). Although Freud's understanding of working through was inexact, the concept forever altered the technique of treatment by putting an end to unrealistic expectations that rapid change should follow "insight."

Some of Freud's heuristically useful theories have fallen into disuse not so much because they have been completely invalidated but as a result of being superseded by hypotheses of wider applicability. The most significant theoretical shift of that kind has been the abandonment of Freud's distinction between enduring functional realms he called *ego* and *id* (1923) as an explanatory tool of universal significance for the understanding of behavior regulation (see Gedo and Goldberg 1973). Freud's tripartite model of mind (ego, id, superego) is still cogent for the identification of intrapsychic conflicts, but such conflicts are no longer viewed as the crux of all psychopathology. In my judgment, maladaptation is best understood as the consequence of inborn or acquired apraxia (see Gedo 1988) or dyspraxia.

The Freudian Legacy

Within psychoanalysis, Freud's prestige remained enormous well beyond his lifetime. As the founder of the discipline, so many of whose ideas proved to be valid and/or fruitful, for many he approached infallibility. Happily, such idealization has gradually disappeared; in contemporary psychoanalysis, each of Freud's specific contributions can generally be assessed on its particular merits. (Those psychoanalysts who cannot dispense with an idealized meister can choose among a number of more recent contributors to put on a pedestal.) I believe psychoanalysis is now ready to give Freud credit *only* where credit is due.

Whether the general public can forgive Freud for his fallibility remains to be seen. It is not unusual for great contributions to go into temporary eclipse with a change in intellectual fashions, and the postmodern era has not been conducive to introspection—or, for that matter, to the *vita contemplativa* as a whole. Yet dark ages are generally followed by a renaissance.

Summary

By devising a novel observational method, Freud could discern certain crucial regularities in mental functioning that had escaped previous scientific attention. The most important of these were (1) that mentation is usually unconscious, (2) that there is a compulsion automatically to repeat previous patterns of thought, feeling, and behavior, (3) that unfortunate experiences in early life have a vital role in personality development by structuring behavioral dispositions, and (4) that there are two distinct modes of thought processing.

Freud felt the scientific obligation to fit his new observations into a coherent theory of mind. Because he understood mentation to be a dependent concomitant of neural activity, he turned to contemporary neurology and theoretical biology to borrow concepts, however imperfect, that could undergird such a "metapsychology." Subsequently, many of the subsidiary clinical concepts of psychoanalysis were, in turn, based on that invalid metapsychology. Their lack of scientific validity has, in the past generation, led to the reconsideration of most aspects of psychoanalytic theory.

CHAPTER TWO

Hermeneutics and Biology in the Psychoanalytic Situation

Although it is widely known that Sigmund Freud was trained in neurology and neurophysiology rather than in psychiatry, the fact that he always viewed mental functions as products of neural activity has received relatively little emphasis from intellectual historians (but see Sulloway 1979). Rather, it has been the fashion to assume that, when in 1895 Freud found that his understanding of brain functions did not suffice to construct a "scientific psychology," he turned to the study of "the mind," divorced from its somatic matrix, notably in chapter 7 of *The Interpretation of Dreams* (Freud 1900). (For a refutation of this historical view, see Kanzer 1973.) However, in order to anchor psychoanalysis within the biological sciences, Freud proposed a speculative "metapsychology" that dealt with postulated drives fueled by psychic energy. As he wrote C. J. Jung (see Jung 1963, 150–51), Freud looked upon these constructs as the essential safeguards against allowing psychoanalysis to slip into vitalism, mentalism, or even occultism—doctrines that view the human soul as a nonmaterial entity.

Although Freud's metapsychological hypotheses did not prove to have clinical relevance or predictive value, on several occasions they have been amended to *conform* to the clinical findings of subsequent generations of analysts; the most significant of these reforms occurred in the work of Heinz Hartmann (1939, 1964; see also Hartmann, Kris, and Loewenstein 1964). Arguably, these theoretical works of Hartmann and those of Rapaport (1959, 1967) marked the end of widespread adherence to the initial biological paradigm within psychoanalytic theory. Schafer (1970) was the first simultaneously to pay tribute to the heuristic value of these theoretical contributions while pronouncing that they had become passé. Further doubts about the epistemic adequacy of Freud's late-nineteenth-century postulates were explicitly stated in the literature about twenty-five years ago (see Swanson 1977; Toulmin 1978). In the mid-1970s, the long-lasting metapsychological consensus collapsed in the face of a variety of cogent arguments. Relatively conservative theoreticians might continue to use the vocabulary of Freud's metapsychology, but (with rare exceptions [see Opatow 1989]) they have acknowledged that, in doing so, they are dealing in metaphors, albeit without conceding that propositions framed as mere metaphors are untestable and therefore, from a scientific viewpoint, they have no precise meaning and cannot be used to undergird a biological framework for psychoanalysis.

On Theoretical Coherence

Throughout the 1970s, the major theoretical thrust within American psychoanalysis was a successful effort, led by many of Rapaport's students (G. Klein 1976; Schafer 1976; Holt 1965, 1967, 1976; Gill 1976) as well as others (Rosenblatt and Thickstun 1977), to discredit Freud's metapsychology (see also Gill and Holzman 1976). Many of these contributors explicitly abandoned the assumption that psychoanalytic theory has to deal with issues beyond mental contents; consequently, they led a broad movement to conceive of psychoanalysis as a purely hermeneutic discipline. (For a recent statement of this view, see Gill 1995.) These American developments were congruent with parallel ones abroad, such as that of the Lacanian school in France (see Muller and Richardson 1982) or those of various British object relations theorists (Fairbairn 1954, Guntrip 1968, Winnicott 1958, 1965). Even the defenders of ego psychology (the metonymic designation of Freud's ultimate theory of mental function) tended to disavow those aspects of Freudian thinking that did not involve intrapsychic conflicts in the form of conscious or unconscious fantasies (see Arlow and Brenner 1964, Brenner 1982)—in other words, they focused on mental contents exclusively.

On the Hermeneutic Challenge

Such a focus on mental contents threatens, in turn, to exclude psychoanalysis from the domain of empirical science because matters of subjectivity lend themselves poorly to study through scientific methods. Thus the tendency to focus on hermeneutics soon resulted in further epistemological objections to the validity of psychoanalytic observations as scientific evidence (most emphatically expressed by Grünbaum [1984]). As stated by respected clinicians (such as Gill 1995; see also Hoffman 1991, 1992), these objections claim that the covert meanings of free associations are never self-evident; they have to be "constructed" through the joint efforts of analyst and analysand. Further, these skeptics believe that the material of the analysand's associations is inevitably skewed by the actual interpersonal transactions within the therapeutic dyad. The most extreme advocates of these caveats (such as Stolorow and Atwood 1992) label their viewpoint one of "intersubjectivity"; these theorists imply that the unavoidable influence of the analytic observer precludes the identification of structured intrapsychic conditions in the observed.

If, as many hermeneuticists would have it, the subject matter of psychoanalysis were restricted to the communications of the analysand (even if these were supplemented by the affective responses of the analyst), the foregoing doubts about the truth value of analytic interpretations would have to be taken extremely seriously. (At the same time, the contentions of those who advocate adoption of a "constructivist" epistemology, such as Gill [1995], that the prevalence of positivism in psychoanalysis has led to the misuse of the interpretive method through arbitrariness and emotional or intellectual bias, are definitely overstated. Proper interpretive technique has always involved testing the validity of the analyst's conjectures by monitoring their effects on the analysand's subsequent associations [see Freud 1937]. These caveats found their ultimate expression in Gardner's [1983] cogent proposal that the task of interpretation is primarily to be performed by the analysand, while that of the analyst is to focus on assisting this effort of self-inquiry. Consensus between analyst and analysand does not guarantee that their joint interpretations will necessarily be valid; it should, however, eliminate the analyst's arbitrariness and bias as sources of error. The multiple meanings of the contents of mind are, however, extremely difficult to decipher.)

It is essential to note that, judging by their clinical reports, even hermeneuticists take their observational data from a field broader than the contents of mind that can be surveyed through introspection and empathy—Kohut's (1959) overly restrictive definition of the purview of psychoanalysis. This shows that psychoanalysis is more than "a purely psychological discipline dealing with human meanings" (Gill 1995, 101). For instance, Stolorow and Atwood (1992, 64–83) discuss the case of a suicidal person who believed that her brother was "a part of her"; they endorse the therapist's conclusion that this belief constituted a delusion and the consequent decision to focus the treatment on an effort to correct this disordered thinking. Such a choice is based on a diagnostic conclusion that privileges the therapist's expertise with regard to cognition and reality testing, and thereby temporarily abandons the "intersubjective" framework.

Gill has also acknowledged that, in certain dangerous contingencies, it is incumbent on the analyst to insist on measures to safeguard all persons concerned; this admission also surrenders the basic principle of constructivism. "Sometimes a directive, a piece of advice, a suggestion about how to behave in a difficult situation may seem desirable to break an impasse or an obsessional vicious circle" (1995, 57). Further, he writes, "To convert what is ego system in the patient to symptomatic status [requires] intervention on the analyst's part. [The analyst has] to insist that the patient's life style is a pathological one before the analysis [can] enter a new phase" (1995, 75).

If the crux of the matter is merely to decide what constitutes a therapeutic emergency, the answer will depend precisely on the analyst's acuity in detecting the potential risk of leaving patients to fend for themselves on the basis of their usual adaptive devices. In other words, analysts must go beyond monitoring the human meanings of their analysands' free associations: they are obliged, in the mode of ethnological observers, to collect data about the overall psychological and psychobiological adaptive repertory of their patients. To use the simplest of examples: it is not only analytically legitimate but vitally important to see to it that an analysand gets appropriate medication to control threatening manic or depressive developments. Admittedly, whenever we come forward as experts, we take the risk of being in error; nonetheless, we cannot avoid the role of natural scientists and, like all other health care providers, the responsibilities of trained and licensed practitioners.

On Psychoanalytic Knowledge and the Biology of the Mind

The constructivist/intersubjective viewpoint turns out to be overstated, for the assumptions of its extremist advocates—that all facts are based on theory and that true knowledge is unattainable—are mere rhetorical exaggerations. In 1492, the assertion that the earth was essentially spherical was an unproved hypothesis; today, it is a fact that does not depend on theory. When one loses a tooth, the observation that this structure is missing is also made without relying on what constructivists call theory. The argument that the very existence of external reality is mere hypothesis is empty, for if it were accepted, even the ordinary business of everyday life would become impossible. Reasonable constructivists do not carry their arguments that far. There is no uncertainty about the beneficial effect of brushing one's teeth. Damage to psychological structure is admittedly more difficult to ascertain, and we do not as yet happen to *know* what measures to recommend to minimize the risks of unfavorable psychological developments. Yet it would be unreasonable to claim that we lack knowledge about the generally destructive consequences of various types of early childhood abuse or misfortunes.

As Stephen Jay Gould (1995) has noted, the human cognitive apparatus has, through evolution, become well adapted to processing those data we need to comprehend in order to cope in everyday life. These do not include theoretical physics or metapsychology, but they do embrace a vast array of observations that can be made in the psychoanalytic situation. The same point was conceded by Schafer (1995, 231): "Those who adopt an absolutist position on intersubjectivity are making claims about knowing, facticity, or reality testing that they cannot totally support in practice. Here I would point especially to those . . . who claim that the analyst is not, and should never try to be, the ultimate authority in the clinical dialogue on what is real, true and correct, or else fantastic, false, or distorted; in other words, to those who claim there can only be encounters of two subjective realities in what is implicitly a completely solipsistic universe."

What the psychoanalytic literature has hitherto failed to stress is that we know little or nothing about the actual significance of any particular set of mental contents. (The point may be restated by saying that almost all fantasies are ubiquitous—or by recalling once again that every interpretive schema proposed in the course of psychoanalytic history has served about as well as every other.) Our painfully accumulated store of analytic knowledge does not concern a differential diagnosis of putatively maladaptive desires or our conflicts about them; it is largely confined, instead, to the significance of the manner in which thoughts (including their affective components) are processed. Thus it is not legitimate to correlate the occurrence of a fantasy of levitation with any particular behavioral constellation, but we are *certain* that anyone who gives credence to such a fantastic idea will suffer severe maladaptive consequences. This judgment is not a matter of establishing "human meanings," in the sense suggested by Gill (1995, 3) of discerning some psychic reality through empathy—rather, it is one of accepting certain laws of nature, with special reference to human biology. This particular bit of knowledge is as old as the hills—witness the myth of Icarus—but only the observational setting of psychoanalysis has permitted detailed examination of the changes in reality testing that determine if and when an individual will be delusional in this manner. (For an illustration of the subtleties of the diagnostic differentiation required, see Sadow and Suslick 1961.)

What psychoanalysts have learned about the regulation of behavior and the biology of mind in the course of a century of clinical work is focused on certain functions of the central nervous system, particularly cognition (including perception) and communication (including affectivity). This is the domain Freud (1895a) made a premature attempt to map out in the *Project for a Scientific Psychology* (see also Levin 1991, Gedo 1996). The Freudian metapsychology we are in the process of discarding (as a metaphor now emptied of heuristic value) was an attempt to hypothesize (through mechanistic and energetic analogies) how the central nervous system might regulate behavior. It is well to recall that, a short generation ago, there was still consensus that a specifically psychoanalytic perspective about human behavior required the concurrent use of what were called "the points of view of metapsychology" (Rapaport and Gill 1959). Theoretical arguments were then centered on whether to accept Hartmann's (1939) proposal of an adaptive viewpoint on a par with the dynamic, genetic, structural, and economic ones used by Freud.

The current antimetapsychological camp in psychoanalysis, including Gill, as well as most object relations theorists and self psychologists, would confine our purview to the consideration of dynamics and genetics—the points of view relevant to the study of mental contents. Such a reduction of our observational field suits the current fashion of assuming that mental life can only be conceived in terms of a "two person psychology." This view involves the misuse of developmental data about the imperative symbiotic needs of infants to make unwarranted inferences about the functioning of adults. (For a detailed discussion of what I consider to be the appropriate place of interpersonal and intrapsychic frames of reference in psychoanalysis, see Gedo 1988, chap. 9; for the undeniable problems posed by "intersubjectivity," see Gedo 1991a, chap. 7).

It is a fascinating paradox that, while they might focus exclusively on the meanings of mental contents, most psychoanalysts take great pains to document their legitimacy by showing that they remain cognizant of human biology ("the body," as the current jargon puts it) by virtue of continued attention to sexuality and aggression. It is true, of course, that sexual and aggressive motives are functions of the soma, but (if we are to avoid postulating a disembodied "soul") so is every other human manifestation. To state this differently, the parts of the body specifically relevant for psychoanalysis are not the genitals or the musculoskeletal system (these are truly worthy of attention only in terms of their "human meanings," à la Gill) but the various components of the central nervous system. Yet the current majority of psychoanalytic authors advocate ignoring the latter. (For some exceptions, see Krystal 1988; Levin 1991, 2003; Modell 1993; Gedo 1991a, 1992, 1996.)

The Biological Observables in the Psychoanalytic Setting

What are some of the crucial psychoanalytic data, beyond mental contents and therefore "beyond interpretation" (Gedo 1993a), that will be left out if we adopt a psychology confined to "human meanings" and a hermeneutic technical approach? The most important of these facts is the potential occurrence of episodes wherein there is an altered state of consciousness and an inability to think in a manner that can be encoded in words. These are the conditions that Freud (1892), following his neurological mentors, called *traumatic*. An excellent clinical description of traumatic states is provided by Greenacre: "Traumatic situations . . . tend to be *disorganizing* in their effect on other activities of the individual. They may result either in states of aimless, frenzied overactivity, sometimes culminating in tantrums of rage or, if the stimulus is acute and focused as well as sudden, it may produce a shock-like, stunned reaction, presenting various degrees of unresponse, inactivity, or torpor" (1967, 288).

Freud discussed these conditions most extensively in his *Introductory Lectures* (1916–17, 273–85), but he frequently referred to them in his earliest psychological works, and he reiterated their fundamental importance in "Inhibitions, Symptoms, and Anxiety" (1926), where he stressed that trauma constitutes a situation of helplessness that the individual must subsequently seek to avoid. In other words, Freud regarded overstimulation—what he also called a state of psychoeconomic imbalance—as the most basic situation of danger. Although he was most interested in such conditions in the 1890s (see Freud 1893, 1895b, 1896a, 1896b; see also Breuer and Freud 1895, especially Breuer's chap. 3, sect. 3), as late as 1923, in "The Ego and the Id," he claimed that potential states of psychoeconomic imbalance form the nidus around which other symptoms are erected in order to avoid traumatization. (Freud articulated the related concept of "actual neurosis" in 1898. For a history of this notion, see Sadow et al. 1967).

The failure to take these biological observations into account is the great-est flaw of a hermeneutic approach because this neglect makes it necessary to account for the formation of symptoms and inhibitions on the basis of further metaphorical constructs, such as "compromise formation." In stating this view, I am leaving the domain of observational data for that of clinical theory. Yet among current authors there is almost complete consensus (but for the dissent of Brenner 1987) about the essential role of "working through" in effecting therapeutic change. As I have already explained (Gedo 1995a, 1995b), the op-erational meaning of this metaphor refers primarily to mastery of the threat of traumatization, through gradual change that makes it unnecessary to resort to inhibitions or symptom formation.[1] Thus any disregard of biological issues (formerly termed psychoeconomic) falsely elevates the elucidation of mental contents into a curative measure. Such a misunderstanding of the crux of ther-apeutic psychoanalysis probably accounts for a large proportion of therapeu-tic failures. Conversely, the crucial significance of quantitative considerations is one of the more plausible explanations for the therapeutic effectiveness of the manifold (and sometimes mutually contradictory) interpretive schemata employed by various psychoanalytic schools, albeit on an explicit level they leave mental *processes* out of consideration.

A second set of highly important biological observations that should be col-lected in the psychoanalytic situation is the recurrence (without trauma) of phenomena referable to the preverbal modes of functioning prevalent in ear-liest life, particularly those involving communication and thought processing. Close attention to episodic lapses into a preverbal state or into resort to proto-linguistic channels of communication may lead to the delineation of focal arrests of development and their potential correction (see Gedo 1996). These regressions undo the developmental achievement recently named *mentaliza-tion* (Fonagy et al. 2002). Analogous repair of faulty cognitive operations will also yield great therapeutic benefits: it is much more important to overcome magical thinking than to deal with the specific subject matter about which the individual thinks in that pathological manner.

The occurrence of such faulty thinking or of a protolinguistic phenomenon (for example, some type of "somatization") is a fact we can observe with rela-tive objectivity; such data are not subject to the epistemological problems cre-ated with regard to mental contents (generally related to the person's histori-cal, social, or interpersonal situation) by the issue of intersubjectivity. That is not to say that the analyst's prior activities are irrelevant to the emergence of such data—but their immediate causation is never as important as the fact that they can occur at all, whatever the context may be. To cite an analogous instance, in the midst of a myocardial infarction, the nature of the precipitating events is not of immediate significance; rather, it is imperative to focus on the current functional problem. (For a clinical illustration, see Gedo 1991b.)

The last example of observable psychoanalytic data "beyond mental contents" I offer here is that of repetitive patterns of behavior in response to transactions in the treatment situation; these enactments may occur within the analytic setting or outside it. (For detailed discussion of such behaviors, see Gedo 1988, chap. 7 and 9.) Freud (1920) was the first to call attention to the compulsive nature of certain repetitive patterns of conduct that do not seem aimed at satisfying any wish: as he put it, they lie "beyond the pleasure principle." The most convincing clinical illustration of such behavior is the "addiction" to painful sensations noted by Valenstein (1973). Probably because Freud understood the phenomena of repetition compulsion in terms of the effects of a putative "death instinct," a formulation that in subsequent years has found almost no acceptance in North America, these phenomena have been widely slighted in clinical discourse. It may be superfluous to spell out that the adoption of a hermeneutically centered technique makes it all but impossible to detect such patterns because these have never been encoded in words.

On Psychoanalytic Treatment as Biological Change

I trust I have discussed the relevant issues in sufficient detail to show that adequate psychoanalytic practice necessarily involves matters beyond the lexical meaning of the analysand's associations. The hermeneutic challenge to a biological conception of psychoanalysis that has arisen in reaction to the exhaustion of Freud's century-old metapsychological paradigm has only been feasible because its proponents have programmatically excluded observable biological phenomena from analytic consideration. At the same time, the constructivist viewpoint, which casts severe doubt on the validity of any a priori interpretation of the meanings of analysands' communications, deserves to be taken seriously. Successful use of every coherent interpretive schema proposed within psychoanalysis suggests that "structural change" depends on factors that lie beyond dealing with mental contents; in this sense, the validity of psychoanalytic interpretations (or the lack of it) is probably epiphenomenal. (For a similar view, see Levenson 1983, Modell 1990).

Elsewhere (Gedo 1988, epilogue), I tried to explain this apparent conundrum through the hypothesis that, whenever interpretation promotes improved adaptation, it does so principally because it makes possible an expansion of the analysand's psychological skills. In other words, consistent interpretations may teach patients how to understand their inner lives so that they may on their own master their propensities for psychoeconomic imbalance and its sequelae. (Note that such mastery does not mean that the interpretations were valid.) I have also proposed (see Gedo 1993a) biological explanations for the effectiveness of the interventions "beyond interpretation" I have advocated for many years (see Gedo and Goldberg 1973, 159–68). Given this record of departures from the theoretical mainstream, it may ill behoove me to use arguments that appeal to the authority of tradition, but, in the present instance, it is desirable to demonstrate how much of the Freudian corpus is abandoned by those who would remove psychoanalysis from the roster of the biological sciences.

When Freud (1923) put forward his structural theory and left behind accessibility of mental contents to consciousness as the primary criterion of adequate adaptation, he was acknowledging that overcoming pathology is a matter of altering the manner in which mental contents are *processed.* The macrostructures of his last theory of mind were to be differentiated not on the basis of the ideas they contain but on that of their distinctive biology. At this stage of Freud's conceptual development, ego and id were characterized by different principles of regulation—the reality principle and the pleasure principle, respectively (see Freud 1911a). In addition, Freud postulated different energetic arrangements for these two systems, so that for him transforming the processing of any content from the manner of the id to that of the ego meant an alteration in biology that was later named "neutralization" (Hartmann 1948). In the vocabulary Freud invented in 1900, "free" cathexes have to be changed into the "bound" variety.[2]

Even if we agree that Freud's metapsychological hypotheses no longer serve our needs, we may not legitimately ignore the issues he tried to address by using them. Whichever theoretical alternative we substitute for Freud's original concepts, the changes brought about by successful treatment will have to be specified in terms of altered psychobiological conditions—developments such as the abandonment of infantile object attachments in favor of mature ones, for instance. Analysts cannot judge these matters on the basis of the analysand's verbal communications alone. Hence the therapist must possess some expertise in order to challenge patients to progress from more primitive to more mature modes of functioning. It is all very well to construct coherent narratives about the analysand's past, but *change* is contingent on teaching an old performer some new tricks. As I have tried to show previously (Gedo 1995a, 1995b), such instruction amounts to the establishment of new functional arrangements in the brain.

In a therapeutic context, it is never adequate merely to discuss "human meanings"—it is also necessary to use those discussions as an opportunity to expand the patient's repertory of psychological skills. We have known for a long time that "love is not enough." It is now time to acknowledge that insight may be necessary, but it is never sufficient. However essential it is accurately to understand analysands' communications in the clinical situation, an exclusive focus on mental contents cannot yield an adequate theory of mental functions, precisely because these are in large measure unconscious and/or lacking in symbolic (verbal) representation.

Summary

The general abandonment of Freud's original metapsychology led many disillusioned psychoanalysts altogether to disregard biology in favor of a purely "mentalist" viewpoint. A corollary of such a decision is to conceive of the analytic procedure as an exclusively hermeneutic enterprise. In practice, however, it proves to be impossible to confine the work to deciphering the meanings of associations. Moreover, the significance (if any) for maladaptation of particular mental contents is not known.

A purely hermeneutic approach leaves out observable variations in human biology, such as the occurrence of trauma, changes in levels of affectivity, resort to primitive thought processes or modes of communication, or wordless enactments. It overlooks that therapeutic change is contingent on alteration in the manner of processing mental contents—often by means of instruction in more effective methods.

CHAPTER THREE

Alternatives to Freud's Biological Theory

Among those who have accepted the need to abandon the metapsychology Freud invented one hundred years ago an irreconcilable difference of opinion has arisen about how to proceed in repairing the resultant shrinkage of psychoanalytic theory into competing sets of clinical propositions—sometimes even into mutually exclusive theoretical fragments simultaneously espoused by one author. (For one example, see Kohut 1977, xvii–xviii.) One faction (including Schafer, G. Klein, and Gill) has maintained that we can make do without metapsychological underpinnings for our clinical theories—in Schafer's (1976) version of this point of view, an experience-near "action language" is deemed most suitable for articulating clinical theory. A second group, best exemplified by Rubinstein (1965, 1967, 1974, 1976), has insisted that theories of unconscious mentation must necessarily resort to neurophysiological explanations, for whatever remains unconscious cannot at the same time be subjectively experienced. In this view, psychoanalysis could not avoid finding a valid alternative to Freud's metapsychology, and biological alternatives to that system were almost within reach. (These arguments, pro and con, were cogently presented in Gill and Holzman 1976.)

Unfortunately, too many psychoanalytic authors ignore questions of theoretical coherence and epistemological respectability, so many recent contributions have simply disregarded the problem. For instance, in the past twenty-five years, Kohut (1977, 1978, 1984) and his followers (e.g., Goldberg 1978) have founded a new school of psychoanalytic thought conforming to the principle that our theories should be as near to personal experience as possible. As a result, the propositions of their "Self Psychology" deal only with issues that can be articulated in the language of subjectivity; in other words, as Modell (1992) has pointed out, they put forward a purely phenomenological theory unconcerned with matters the subject is unable to describe verbally.

Kohut's work deals only with the experiences of what he called a *cohesive self;* he barely noted that this postulated developmental stage is of necessity preceded by one in which such "cohesion" is lacking, a state capable of subjective recurrence in adulthood in the form of what Kohut (1971) called *fragmentation.* Kohut's clinical theory has remained noncommittal on all questions concerning the effects of the earliest phases of development on later psychological life. Moreover, although Kohut explicitly abandoned Freud's "experience distant" metapsychology, Self Psychology has continued to use certain concepts (such as *transmuting internalization*) that only make sense as components of that metapsychology. (What is putatively "transmuted" while internalization takes place would have to be the infantile nature of the patient's mentation.) So much for theoretical coherence. However, a concern with internal consistency and inclusiveness in theory formation, such as this book aims for, has only been expressed among the heirs of Heinz Hartmann—neither Kleinians nor Lacanians (to mention only the most prominent analytic schools) have bothered to address such issues.

The past twenty-five years of psychoanalysis have been characterized by a lack of theoretical consensus, caused by adherence to one of several mutually incompatible epistemological premises (see Gedo 1986, 1999, chap. 19; Grossman 1976, 1984). This is not the place to classify the many significant competing viewpoints in terms of these basic a priori commitments, but I should mention that I have been an active participant in these controversies and that, in agreement with Rubinstein, I have insisted that "depth psychology" is a branch of biological science, whether or not one explicitly acknowledges it. At the very least, every school of psychoanalysis uses some theory of motivation, necessarily rooted in biology. In my view, even vitalist or occultist theories contain (of course, without making it explicit) certain assumptions about "the nature of things"—in other words, any clinical theory in psychoanalysis unavoidably uses some sort of metapsychology, despite the refusal of numerous theoreticians to articulate theirs. Take, for instance, arbitrary assertions such as the Lacanian hypothesis that the Unconscious is structured like a language (see Muller and Richardson 1982). For all we know, this conjecture may be on the mark, but, considering that we have no direct access to anything unconscious, it is founded not on evidence but on a priori assumptions: it goes beyond psychology. It is propositions of this kind that Freud calls *meta-psychological.*

On the Purview of Psychoanalysis

Instead of further elaborating the recent intellectual history of psycho-analysis (but see Gedo 1999), let me consider a related issue. It is frequently claimed (e.g., Gill 1981) that theories about matters that cannot be observed in the psychoanalytic situation have no practical significance for the discipline. To begin with, if such assertions were taken at face value, it would entail re-ducing the purview of psychoanalysis to overt behaviors and conscious men-tal contents communicated through free association. It would also entail the abandonment of all psychoanalytic constructs, even such indispensable no-tions as transference or repression because these involve hypothetical com-mitments that go a long way beyond our clinical observations. (These issues are further discussed in chaps. 4 and 9, respectively.) From this viewpoint, among those who repudiated the use of an explicit metapsychology, only Schafer (1976) proposed an alternative theory that did not illegitimately con-tinue to use the traditional constructs that had allegedly been discarded. His proposals have had little acceptance in large measure because clinicians can-not dispense with these familiar constructs, however suspect they have become on epistemological grounds.

Of course, from a pragmatic viewpoint, it is perfectly feasible (and clinically preferable) to conduct psychoanalyses without resorting to theoretical jargon. The theory of technique espoused by the great majority of analysts holds that our crucial therapeutic tool *is* interpretation of the meanings of the analysand's associations and of behaviors observable in the psychoanalytic situation. As I have mentioned, these interpretations are invariably guided by theories, de-veloped over the course of a century of clinical experience with the psycho-analytic method. These theories deal with psychological development and its vicissitudes, pathogenesis, and even with the general functions we call *men-tal.* Because various schools of psychoanalysis radically differ about all these matters, it is logical and creditable that, for most clinical contingencies, they advocate mutually incompatible interpretive schemata.

With the passage of time, one would have thought that even in the absence of reliable follow-up studies the superiority of the most valid interpretive schema over its rivals might become apparent. It is therefore quite remarkable that nothing of the sort has happened—witness the lack of resolution of the controversy over Melanie Klein's (1984) interpretive schema, a dispute that has continued to smolder for some seventy-five years. As dispassionate observers have noted (e.g., Joseph 1985), there is no evidence that the Kleinians' results are better or worse than those of other schools. It has become a commonplace that there are better and worse clinicians within each of the half-dozen major psychoanalytic schools—in other words, clinical results cannot be predicted on the basis of the analyst's ideology (see also Levenson 1983).

What can this apparent paradox mean? Those of us who are truly confident that we possess psychoanalytic truth tend to assert that those who do not agree with us manage to obtain good results only because of "the therapeutic effects of inexact interpretation"—a phrase invented by Glover (1931) in the hope of exorcising the Kleinian devils that he thought had invaded the body of psychoanalysis. I do not deny that Glover's explanation for the beneficial effects of invalid interventions may sometimes be correct; I merely insist that it is equally effective in casting doubt on the validity of every conceivable interpretive schema. We must therefore face the disturbing fact that psychoanalytic theories cannot be scientifically validated from within psychoanalysis alone; competing analytic hypotheses will also have to be judged on the basis of their congruence with data from cognate fields, such as semiotics, cognitive psychology, and brain science. It would be even better if they were based in the first place on valid knowledge from these relevant disciplines.

On the Mode of Action of Psychoanalysis

The success of treatments based on the interpretive schemata of competing schools of psychoanalysis shows that therapeutic benefits do not primarily depend on the *content* of the interpretation offered; in other words, the subject matter of discussions of mental contents is largely epiphenomenal and obscures other transactions that have greater weight in determining therapeutic outcome. For some time, certain voices within psychoanalysis have asserted as much: Balint's paper of 1932, codifying the ultimate views of Ferenczi, was probably the first explicit statement to this effect. Balint had some influence on the British school of object relations theorists, some of whom have also taught that psychoanalysis succeeds insofar as it creates a novel relationship. In the United States, Loewald (1960) was the first overt exponent of this viewpoint.

Among those of us who believe that our therapeutic effectiveness is based on factors "beyond interpretation" (Gedo 1993a), however, there are further wide differences of opinion on the specifics of the transactions that promote change. Most authors of this persuasion have extrapolated from the late work of Ferenczi (summarized by Bacon and Gedo 1993) to articulate hypotheses that assume that a novel kind of human relationship provided by the therapist automatically promotes a corrective experience (cf. Alexander and French 1946). The self psychologists' emphasis on the necessity of doing analysis within an "empathic ambience" (Wolf 1976, 1992) is one illustration of recent hypotheses of this kind.

As I have elsewhere spelled out in greater detail (Gedo 1993b), in certain cases such a prescription is more or less effective, but in many others it will not suffice, for structured mental dispositions often make it impossible for analysands to make proper use of the unprecedented mode of relating that the treatment offers. (One familiar example of such a contingency is the frequent occurrence of therapeutic impasse based on some countertransference evoked through "projective identification" [M. Klein 1952].) In summary, the provision neither of consistent interpretations nor that of a benign new relationship can in every case explain the therapeutic effectiveness of the psychoanalytic method.

Among those who have proposed broader explanations of the therapeutic action of psychoanalysis, Gardner (1983) has been most persuasive. He has pointed out that the need to clarify the significance of mental contents is unending, so no amount of interpretive work during the analysis can suffice to forestall the recurrence of difficulties unless the analysand learns to process his or her own associations in a manner that will illuminate their meanings. Hence, in Gardner's view, the principal function of the analyst's interpretive activity is to teach the analysand how to arrive at valid interpretations.

In agreement with Gardner's thesis, I have proposed that therapeutic effectiveness depends on instructing patients in a manner that will assist them to acquire hitherto missing psychological skills of various kinds (Gedo 1988, 211–26; see also Wilson and Weinstein 1992). In other words, I contend that the ability to make interpretations is only one example of a whole class of necessary mental functions that may be acquired in the course of effective analytic treatment. Shane and Shane (1995) have implicitly endorsed this claim in writing that analytic cure depends on analysands actively learning to establish human relationships of a kind hitherto inaccessible to them. As I have previously stated (Gedo 1995b), learning to relate more effectively implies prior improvement of various aspects of thinking—to mention only the most obvious among these, an ability to differentiate current experience from expectations based on memories.

In past psychoanalytic discourse, learning processes of these kinds have been recognized under the rubric of "working through" (Gedo 1995a). This metaphor refers to a variety of psychological changes beyond the realm of mental contents—the acquisition of better *modes* of thinking about various particular issues. In my experience, such changes fall into four principal categories: (1) mastery of the propensity to get disorganized (i.e., traumatized) when confronted with intense stimulation, (2) expansion of "referential activity" (Bucci 1993) (i.e., the correlation of primary and secondary thinking processes), (3) increasing tolerance for the intensity of affects, and (4) the acquisition of hitherto missing skills in interpersonal and intrapsychic communication. Teaching analysands to interpret the significance of their associations is the clearest possible example of the expansion of referential activity—and of enhanced intrapsychic communication.

It is well to recall that Freud (1920) viewed the tendency to repeat maladaptive behaviors as a biological attribute—in 1926, he classified such phenomena as manifestations of "id resistance." In his theoretical universe, these matters were dealt with in terms of the economic and structural points of view, in contrast to the dynamic and genetic viewpoints employed to consider mental contents. Cognitive competence is, indeed, largely biologically determined, but it is not legitimate to assume, as Freud did more than eighty years ago, that it is a matter based on drive constitution alone—a point Hartmann (1939) long ago tried to demonstrate. In fact, whatever the etiology of less than optimal thought processing may be, such an apraxia constitutes the stabilization of certain functional arrangements in the central nervous system; these can only change through the gradual building up (or *structuralization,* to use a psychoanalytic synonym) of alternative neural pathways.[1] This is the ultimate reason for the slow rate of "structural change" in the course of analytic treatment, however accurate the analyst's interpretations of mental contents may be. (This is not to say that analysts need not concern themselves with the validity and relevance of their interpretations, for invalid or irrelevant interventions are not likely to help analysands usefully to expand their cognitive repertory.)

If the successes of psychoanalysis-as-treatment therefore depend on teaching patients to use more effective modes of thinking, we must conclude that theories narrowly focused on dynamic-genetic constellations are seriously misleading and their employment will almost inevitably lead to the adoption of relatively unhelpful technical measures. For instance, any theory based exclusively on the construction of meaningful life narratives would tend to discourage analytic concern about propensities for traumatization or a paucity of referential activity, and so forth. I judge this to be the case because narratives naturally focus on interpersonal relations rather than on their ultimate consequences in the internal milieu—least of all on the biological predispositions that codetermine those consequences.

Brenner's (1987) refusal to acknowledge that "working through" consists of anything beyond consistent and valid interpretive activity represents only one among the numerous analytic viewpoints that reduce their purview to the realm of mental contents. Ironically, Self Psychology adopts the same reductionist position, despite its insistence that an empathic ambience is therapeutically more important than the provision of insight. I reach this conclusion because true empathy presupposes a valid understanding of the analysand's interpersonal situation, which, in turn, can only be assessed on the basis of the constellation of mental contents.

Whatever their epistemological shortcomings may have been, Freud's metapsychological propositions at least did respond to the crucial *questions* about psychopathology and its treatment. Whether encoded in the early aphorism to make the unconscious conscious or in its replacement, "Where id was, there shall ego be" (Freud 1933, 80), Freud's hypotheses made clear that the functional changes we must strive for in analysis involve profound alterations in human biology. He was well aware that *naming* mental contents that have been unconscious does not suffice to raise them to consciousness (Freud 1915b)—that extending the realm he called ego to previously inaccessible functional units he classified as id requires difficult changes in *processing* the contents of mind, such as replacing behavior regulated by the pleasure principle with that under the sway of the reality principle, or managing to transcend the compulsion to repeat (Freud 1920, 1923). Because changes of this kind do not automatically take place after the acquisition of insight, Freud postulated that additional psychoeconomic vectors are at work in effecting structural change— a viewpoint best articulated by Hartmann (1964, 164–81) in a paper on *neutralization*, the putative taming of unbound psychic energy.

It is no coincidence that many theorists who have, on epistemological grounds, abandoned the postulate of psychic energy but do not feel that there is a need to find a substitute for Freud's metapsychology, such as Gill (1981), are ready to confine the subject matter of psychoanalysis to matters of subjectivity (more recently, *intersubjectivity*). In this regard, Gill concurs with Kohut and his followers. The one proposal from the antimetapsychological camp for a coherent theoretical substitute, Schafer's (1976) action language, makes absolutely no provision for the "daemonic" forces Freud attributed to the human depths; in Schafer's proposed language, there was no passive voice. In other words, he made no room in his theory for biological events such as trauma, emptiness, disorganization, confusion, or helplessness. If mental life were, indeed, confined to the realm encompassed by action language, there would be no reason to provide psychoanalytic theory with a biological matrix, and a classification of narratives would suffice to explicate human psychology.

On Psychoanalysis and Brain Science

As I have already mentioned, it was Rubinstein (1974, 1976) who, in papers published more than twenty-five years ago, spelled out what kind of biological foundations are needed by a psychoanalysis that aspires to scientific status. (It is important to recall that many psychoanalysts, including most of the French, reject the need to give psychoanalysis scientific credibility; as I understand their position, they regard the discipline as a philosophically based way of life, essentially an inheritor of the traditions of the various schools of Greco-Roman philosophy. Instead of seeking empirical support, adherents of such an intellectual doctrine generally seem most concerned with the prima facie persuasiveness of their propositions. It is no coincidence that French psychoanalytic ideas are extremely popular among scholars of the humanities, who are generally uninterested in the evidence available to back or refute psychoanalytic notions.)

When Rubinstein did his work, contemporary brain science was almost as unserviceable for his purposes as it had been in 1895, when Freud failed in the attempt to outline a "scientific psychology." Consequently, Rubinstein hypothesized what he called a "proto-neurophysiology"—a mere model of the kind of concrete neurophysiological information needed to explicate the psychic operations relevant for psychoanalysis. In the past two decades, there has been an explosion of information about the functioning of the central nervous system, the relevant parts summarized for psychoanalysts by authors such as Reiser (1984), Levin (1991, 2003), Hadley (1985, 1989, 1992, 2000), Schwartz (1987), Basch (1976), Schore (1994), and others.

It is not my goal to characterize this massive body of information here; I merely wish to record that it contains much of the data on which understanding of behavior regulation in the preverbal era of infancy must be based.

Psychoanalytic theory has to include valid propositions about the regulation of behavior in the preverbal era and during the developmental phases that follow the acquisition of symbolic capacities; moreover, it has to be able to explicate the transition from the earlier mode of regulation to the later one, as well as any regressive retreat to prevalence of the earlier mode. In other words, only theories that parallel the hierarchical arrangement of the central nervous system (cf. Hughlings Jackson 1884) are sufficiently inclusive and flexible to do justice to the complexity of human behavior. A number of theories that meet these criteria have been proposed (see Wilson and Gedo 1993), including one of my own (Gedo 1988, 1991a, 1993a).

I do not propose to go into detail concerning the relative advantages or disadvantages of the various extant hierarchical theories. Suffice it to say that, as Grossman (1993) has shown, Freud's theory of mind always took cognizance of the hierarchical arrangement of behavior regulation. In order to qualify as a biological theory (rather than an arbitrary and untestable philosophical doctrine), psychoanalytic psychology must *at a minimum* be correlated with the parallel hierarchies constructed to illuminate human communication, cognition, and (ultimately) the organization of the central nervous system.

I conclude this chapter by returning to one of the pragmatic consequences of failing to anchor psychoanalytic theory to prevailing knowledge about the organization of the neural substrate subserving mental functions. When these matters are disregarded, we tend to extrapolate from the psychic life of adults to that of young children in a manner that overlooks the lack of input from the prefrontal cortex in the latter. This leads to absurdities such as postulating the operation in infants of "unconscious fantasies" involving conceptual categories (most often judgments of "good" and "bad") and their articulation by means of systems of symbols (M. Klein 1984). Just as frequently, it leads to the assumption that human psychological problems can always be reduced to the presence of intrapsychic conflicts (Wurmser 1994), instead of acknowledging that conflict implies the ability to maintain past psychological goals when confronted with novel circumstances—a considerable developmental achievement, contingent on maturation of the frontal lobes. Many other instances could be cited.

Insofar as psychoanalysts attempt to deal with problems that stem from early arrests of development (A. Freud 1965) or, a fortiori, derailment of development in the preoedipal era, the conflicts they encounter in clinical work stem from relatively late efforts to ward off the archaic mentality left in the wake of these early vicissitudes. Of course, to obtain satisfactory results in treatment, such conflicts must be dealt with, but in these difficult cases they do not constitute the primary psychopathology, which consists of continuing primitiveness in thought processing, such as alexithymia (Krystal 1988) or other forms of apraxia (Gedo 1988). The primitive regulation of behavior takes place on a biopsychological basis radically different from the mental universe of children endowed with the capacity to communicate through consensual language. Psychoanalytic theories divorced from neurophysiological (especially neurocognitive) considerations encourage the disastrous technical prescription to deal with all patients as if they possessed the "intact ego" Eissler (1953) long ago showed to be a theoretical fiction. (The lamentable outcomes this leads to are documented in Wallerstein 1986.)

Summary

Because the differing interpretive schemata of competing schools of psychoanalysis yield essentially similar results, the curative factor in treatment cannot be the provision of any particular information. Analogously, the opportunity to form a new relationship with a benign analyst does not lead to predictable results. In Freudian discourse, the poorly understood curative measures that actually produce change were metaphorically described as a process of "working through."

Successful analytic intervention has to effect permanent changes in the patient's biology. This task, in turn, involves dealing with the hierarchical arrangement of the central nervous system. Psychopathology generally means less than optimal development within the earlier phases of that structuralization, often in the era preceding the acquisition of symbolic capacities. Hence the most important maladaptive dispositions are not verbally encoded and will be overlooked by an exclusively hermeneutic focus.

CHAPTER FOUR

The Psychoanalytic Import of Mental Contents

Transference as Resistance

Although an exclusive focus on the meaning of mental contents would eliminate the crux of psychoanalysis (its insistence on the centrality of unconscious processes for proper understanding of psychopathology and its remediation), any neglect of the hermeneutic dimension of analytic clinical work also constitutes reductionism that interferes with therapeutic effectiveness. To comprehend why, it may be helpful to review the history of Freud's initial treatment efforts.

In the 1890s, his central theoretical assumption was that psychological treatment either has to help patients master (recent) traumatic events or it has to overcome defensive avoidance of affective storms (Freud 1894, 1896a). These assumptions proved to be therapeutically effective in certain instances (see Breuer and Freud 1895), but in cases where treatment had to go on for some time Freud was often thwarted by his patients' lack of cooperation. (He reported a prototypical encounter of that kind in 1905c.) In time, Freud realized that such uncooperativeness denoted some irrational personal reaction on the part of patients toward him—reactions that repeated patterns of childhood transactions with caretakers. His conclusion may be summed up in the aphorism that the past had somehow cast its shadow upon the present. Freud called this process *transference*.

The lawful occurrence of transference-as-resistance at first cast doubt on the feasibility of psychological intervention as a widely applicable treatment method. Freud was extraordinarily ingenious to have decided that, after such transferences have emerged, the interpretation that they constitute the automatic repetition of a childhood relational pattern would overcome the resistance (1911–1915). Although he cautioned (1914a) that by itself insight does not lead to cure—that an additional process of "working through" is necessary, presumably to master the affective concomitants of transference—thenceforth psychoanalysts became preoccupied with the daunting task of accurate, timely, and appropriately tactful transference interpretation.

To clarify that success in that enterprise is a sine qua non of analytic treatment, I offer a published instance wherein failure to deal interpretively with transference-resistance led to disruption of the analysis (Friedman 1991). I have chosen this example because the analyst is now deceased, and I had the opportunity to discuss it with her. She then amplified the published version by disclosing that the analysand had actually left treatment as a result of the stalemate.[1]

The impasse occurred in the seventh year of a difficult analysis. In a move the analyst regarded as a sign of progress, the patient had recently abandoned a relationship of masochistic bondage to a man. That inappropriate subjection had allegedly persisted because the analysand experienced severe guilt about the prospect of separating from her lover. Indeed, after she left him, the patient for many months engaged in self-destructive behaviors that the analyst regarded as acts of expiation. The analyst's focus on these putatively self-punitive behaviors had no mitigating effect, and it did not occur to her that a transference-resistance had supervened. Instead, the analysand succeeded in persuading her that the behaviors in question were merely natural consequences of her life situation. (We might say that the intrapsychic focus necessary to perceive transference developments had been lost.)

During the stalemate, the analytic material consisted of obsessive preoccupation with a new relationship to a man and its putative hopelessness because of the patient's manifold shortcomings or those of the beloved. The analyst persevered with the previously understood genesis of the analysand's feelings of inadequacy in the context of her father's unreasonable expectations for her; interpretations concentrated, ineffectively, on differentiating the present relationship to a man from the childhood past. (Although these interpretations did not deal with the analytic relationship, they did deal with a transference and were almost certainly correct per se.) The analyst never considered the probable meaning of the patient's litany of misery as an oblique appeal for a maternal response.

In failing to apprehend the transference significance of the analysand's lengthy enactment, within the analytic situation, of some forgotten scenario from the past, the analyst fell into the complementary enactment of the role of an ineffectual mother. Both participants in the transaction repeated an aspect of the analysand's childhood past in the guise of a pantomime. (I prefer to call such eventualities *dyadic enactments.*) While these crucial transactions unrolled, the verbal interchange between the participants was almost devoid of significance.

The first hint of the actual meaning of the situation consisted of the analysand's articulation of the fear that the analyst was opposed to her new love affair. Unfortunately, the analyst did not pursue the significance of this implausible fantasy; instead, she began to experience conscious feelings of "acute frustration at not being able to help [the patient] with her ongoing anxiety." (In experiencing a reaction that would be appropriate for a maternal figure during early childhood, the analyst abandoned a therapeutic role; her "countertransference" could and should have alerted her to the analysand's unconscious transferential expectations.)

The displacement of anxiety from the analytic relationship to that with the new lover continued: the patient began to express concern that she would lose her identity if she allowed herself to become close to this man. The analyst did not wonder whether such anxiety might also be applicable to the analytic situation. Nonetheless, the patient began to show anger because "analysis . . . was too consuming and unending." Even at that juncture, the analyst failed to grasp that a negatively toned maternal transference (presumably referable to early childhood) was in evidence. Consequently, the analysand continued to insist that she, the patient, was bad and crazy—a judgment amply justified in view of her transferential hostility and self-destructiveness. As if to exculpate herself of responsibility for this impasse, the analyst in her published report asserted that her patient "clung" to these opinions that, in the analyst's view, were irrational. In other words, the analyst insisted that the analysand must improve her adaptation without having had the benefit of accurate transference interpretation.

These issues were never dealt with while the analysis continued, and the treatment was interrupted—although, in the analyst's view (and even that of the patient), work remained to be done. (Analysands have innumerable ways of simultaneously expressing hostility and self-destructiveness.)

Although the analyst's performance in this example was certainly below par, it is never easy to make accurate transference interpretations. It is particularly difficult when (as in this case) the analyst has no relevant information about the childhood past—data often never encoded in verbal form. To show that such obstacles can be overcome, thereby clearing the way for significant expansion of the scope of the analysis, I offer another case summary. This is an excerpt from an analysis I conducted decades ago about which I kept unusually detailed written records.

The potential impasse occurred after two years of analysis during which various aspects of a father-transference had had to be dealt with. The analysis as a process seemed to be going well, albeit few significant adaptive changes had apparently taken place. Perhaps the most important overt improvement was increasing tolerance for feelings of guilt, with a resultant decrease in expiatory self-destructive behaviors.

For no reason that I could grasp, the patient abruptly withdrew into somnolence on the couch. She claimed that sleeping in my presence constituted engaging in behavior that she had had no opportunity to enjoy with her father. This conjecture was soon disproved: she began to be overtly uncooperative, for instance, by talking so softly that I could not hear her. I was completely bewildered and felt helpless. Finally I hazarded the conjecture that she was trying to reduce me to a state of helpless anger.[2] Her provocativeness escalated, and now she showed flashes of unprecedented anger: "Going to sleep is the most insulting thing I can do to you; it's worse than a slap in the face." She reveled in her power to withhold her associations; she was open about wanting to revenge herself on me—as she revealed, to my complete surprise, for thwarting her wishes for omnipotence! When I characterized her behavior as that of a defiant child, the patient enacted that role even more intensely: "It's a great triumph to see one can enrage someone." However, she did ask her older sister for information about her behavior in early childhood, and she learned that she had been a spoiled and willful favorite, an "abominable child." In the present, she had been trying to reproduce that status through the conviction that she was irresistible to men; my dispassionate responses to her deflated her omnipotent fantasy and produced her limitless anger and her (now conscious) efforts to torture me.

Interpreting such material in the context of the father transference (much as the analyst of the other case had done with her patient) generally led to temporary cessation of these unruly enactments, even to reasonable assessments about the dynamics involved, only to yield to recurrence of the "misbehavior." It took me some time to realize that the emergence of the infantilism represented analytic progress, the uncovering of the analysand's true self, previously concealed by a spurious facade of passivity and sweetness. What soon followed was clarification of the patient's insistent demand for continuous positive feedback.

Thus, undoing the transference-resistance by interpretation did not lead to adaptive change; it merely opened the door to exploration of the analysand's narcissistic problems. To put this another way, it enabled us to deal with those of her problems that had their genesis prior to the age of four. She was terrified about what she would experience in that regard and did her best to escape those potentialities by disrupting our analytic alliance. Several cycles of uncooperativeness followed. Gradually, we came to realize that they were reactions to actual or potential separations. My interpretations now began to focus on the mother transference, and this led to a fruitful termination phase for the analysis. (The outcome of this treatment was unusually successful, confirmed by a follow-up almost forty years later.)

I hope this summary gives sufficient information to show that effective management of transference-resistance via interpretation is sometimes feasible. Yet in itself such interpretation has no curative effect. How could it have led to improved adaptation, considering that it did not address any actual psychopathology? None of the phenomena that appeared in the analytic situation as transference-resistance were characteristic of the patient's usual adult behavior—these were childhood patterns that had been transcended in the course of development. She had not sought analytic treatment because she longed to be cherished as someone's "silly pumpkin" (to quote her explanation for her grievance against me); she needed help because she was unable to cope with certain practical necessities of adult existence.

Transferences in analysis can best be understood as emergent memories, encoded not in words but as action patterns. From a biological perspective, they amount to the classification of current perceptions in terms of long-established categories. As Levin (2003, chaps. 3 and 5) has pointed out, although such a tendency leads to occasional errors, in most instances it is adaptively very efficient. Consequently, transferences are ubiquitous and not pathological per se. (From a pragmatic viewpoint, analysts can fruitfully ask themselves about the transference significance of any and all behaviors of their analysands.) The emergence of a particular transference pattern in treatment, if correctly understood as a reflection of a past without representation in consciousness, actually makes possible the reconstruction of the psychological world of childhood (Freud 1937).

If transference-resistance is consistently overcome through accurate interpretation, analysands are enabled to learn all sorts of things in a variety of ways. Here is one example from the second year of the analysis I have just summarized. The patient started her associations, after spending an unusually quiet, solitary weekend, in this way: "I never realized before that one can look at a person, anybody, find that person sexually attractive, and think about it. That that is the way people normally perceive each other. . . I know that this change is, in a way, a surrender to your way of doing things. I am going to relax and let whatever comes come. You have somehow brainwashed me."

Actually, we had never discussed this matter—I assume she acquired this important bit of know-how by identifying with my medical attitude of never responding to her sexuality, either with denial of its potency or by erotic arousal. (Similarly, in the follow-up session forty years later, she noted that one of the most valuable things she had learned from me was the need for financial prudence. I was astonished: this practical matter had never come up for explicit consideration either.)

For this analysand, it was not easy to accept another person's mode of thinking. Immediately after reporting that I had had real influence on her, she dreamt that her purse had been stolen and she lost her identification. She understood this to mean that learning from me constituted a threat to her very identity. She then quoted Antoine de St. Exupéry to the effect that what is essential is invisible: the curative power of psychoanalysis is effected on an unconscious level. She was unusually clear about how the treatment could help her, and she did not regard insight as the road to improvement. For example, she said, about her tendency unrealistically to idealize men, "If I became close to someone, if I learned to depend on him and love him, and then I would gradually come to see his faults, I could correct my beliefs. I could learn to see reality." This is the curative process that I later proposed to call *optimal disillusionment* (Gedo and Goldberg 1973).

Well into the third year of this analysis, I became unduly discouraged because there was no change in the patient's fantasy life. When I told her that she always returned to the same preoccupations, she emphatically corrected me: "Everything has changed! When I feel I am having a secret love affair with you, I know the fantasy is not sensible. I am grateful to you because you are reliable—you are always there. I can't imagine not coming here, and I know that I'll only be well when I can stop on my own initiative. I don't hate you any more for needing you."

Note that all of the improvements the patient rightly looked upon as significant had to do with newly acquired methods of *processing* mental contents. To use a computer analogy, she was using programs previously unavailable to deal with the same old mental contents: she was now able to reject omnipotent thoughts as "not sensible," and she could tolerate a relationship that she did not totally control. (As she had already stated, she would, on the basis of the ability not to withdraw from such a situation, gain the opportunity to de-idealize parental figures.)

As mentioned in chapter 3, better reality testing and greater affect and frustration tolerance (the crux of the adaptive changes described in this example) are changes in basic biological functions. These can only take place through the gradual establishment of new arrangements within the central nervous system—functional changes not confined to the cerebral cortex but involving midbrain and cerebellar connections as well. (For the neurophysiology of affect regulation, see Schore 1994; for the role of the cerebellum, see Levin 1991; for that of the limbic system, see Levin 2003.)

Transference as Facilitator of Therapy

It may seem paradoxical that, while interpretation of transference reactions does not in itself constitute a curative measure, analytic treatment apparently cannot be effective if no transference emerges in its course. When this empirical finding became evident, ten to fifteen years after Freud began to use the psychoanalytic method, analyzable disorders were, for some time, called the *transference neuroses;* those in which psychoanalysis proved to be unsuccessful were deemed *narcissistic neuroses* (Freud 1914b), on the assumption that these patients were too self-involved to develop transferences vis-à-vis the analyst. (In more recent terminology, such conditions have often been called *schizoid.*)

Further clinical experience showed that the foregoing nosological distinction was oversimplified—note, for instance, that the analysand I describe earlier in this chapter used narcissistic withdrawal to avoid disappointments, but that did not foreclose the emergence of transferences. (Such internal inconsistencies in behavior can be attributed to the "splitting" of mental functions into uncorrelated clusters [Gedo and Goldberg 1973].)

When, after World War II, psychoanalytic theory was used to develop psychotherapeutic techniques different from standard psychoanalysis (defined as the use of free association in a treatment conducted at a frequency of at least four sessions per week), the superior results of psychoanalysis proper were ascribed to the fact that in other forms of therapy transference developments are optimally nipped in the bud through prompt differentiation of the present from the past (Tarachow 1963). By contrast, Freud recommended that transference be allowed to flower—as a possible potentiator of treatment (for instance, because the analysand might wish to please the analyst-qua-parent)—unless it became a resistance to further exploration (Freud 1915a).[3]

A full-fledged transference reaction almost always raises the level of emotional intensity of the analysand's experience; it stirs up childhood passions. An analysis that is making adequate progress becomes a stirring ambience for both participants. Let me illustrate by quoting an interchange from one of the emotional crises of the analysis I have been describing:

> Following a weekend interruption, the patient reported a dream in which she felt that the present weekend would be her last. "In other words, I was going to commit suicide. Then I thought, in the remaining time, why not go to Italy?"
>
> She talked about having been terribly upset since our last session: "I felt alone; I just felt empty. I had no father; I cried. The pain is as bad as if I were having the most terrible physical illness . . . I was so frantic, I almost took [suicidal] action . . . I dreamt of another Italian trip. [During the last one,] when I saw the Pope at the Vatican, I cried."
>
> I interjected, "It's like having contact with your father in heaven."
>
> "Yes! I want to go back . . . I wouldn't want to miss a minute here. It's curious: in the dream, although I was going to Italy, I was still going to have my appointments here."
>
> "So Italy is the analysis, and I am a substitute for your father, like the Pope." (This woman assumed that I am Italian.)
>
> "That's true. On Saturday it seemed so far from the last hour to the next one— I felt so far from a father."
>
> And so on.

Because transference reactions may raise the emotional temperature of the analysis in this manner, Freud (1900, chap. 7) concluded that what got "transferred" in their course was the untamed psychic energy of unconscious mentation. As I have stated in chapter 1, this hypothesis has become untenable; the emotional intensity of full-fledged transferences is actually an echo of affectively charged transactions in childhood. (That such affective reliving is a prerequisite of analytic success was first emphasized by Ferenczi [Ferenczi and Rank 1923]).

This empirical finding brings me back to the apparent paradox that, despite the necessity of living through transference experiences, insight into the meaning of these is not curative. Why, then, do transference reactions promote analytic success? The answer is to be found in the biology of learning: emotional arousal facilitates setting up new neural networks. (For detailed evidence for this conclusion, see Levin 2004.)

It has long been a matter of clinical consensus among psychoanalysts that good results largely depend on the analysand's ability to experience affects. Character types who tend to "intellectualize" or otherwise ward off their emotionality are notoriously difficult to treat, even if the mental contents they report involve transferences. Such affect-poor individuals have usually already suppressed their emotionality in early childhood, so that their transference reactions repeat experiences that were from the first lacking in affectivity. I say more in chapter 9 on affects; here it suffices to restate that cognitive insight alone cannot improve adaptation, and altering any pathology of affectivity is a biological issue independent of any specific mental content.

Transference as Therapeutic Bedrock

Psychoanalysts were somewhat slow to realize that the very willingness of potential analysands to entrust themselves to a therapist had to be based on transference. The conclusion that transference is not a pathological process quietly penetrated into analytic discourse in the guise of "the unobjectionable positive transference"—the expectation, based on past experience, that *caretakers* are, other things being equal, competent, reliable, and *caring*. The term *unobjectionable* actually constituted a misnomer, for this "basic trust" (Benedek 1973) is a *sine qua non* for the establishment of the "analytic alliance" that makes collaboration conceivable. Winnicott (1960) formulated the notion that, in order to succeed, analysis must constitute a "holding environment" for the analysand. (The metaphor alludes to the mother holding a babe-in-arms.)

If a person's earliest experiences have not led to the prevalence of an attitude of basic trust, no effort on the part of the analyst, no matter how ingenious and/or well-intentioned, can establish a holding environment. Such people, if they start analysis, may be able to persevere on the basis of splitting off their fear and mistrust; the traumatized true self at first remains inaccessible, while the analysis engages only a "false self" (Winnicott 1954) acquired in the posttraumatic era of childhood. Needless to say, therapeutic success depends on the emergence, in the context of some kind of archaic transference, of the disavowed true self. Management of the resultant transference-resistance is possible only if, over time, the analyst has shown reliability, competence, and goodwill sufficient to counterbalance the acute negative transference. In that regard, one never knows how much proof is enough.

Whenever transference expectations are predominantly unfavorable from the first, affected individuals seldom seek and persevere with analytic assistance. If they do come for a consultation, their suspicion and lack of candor often evoke negative countertransference responses that fulfill their dire private prophecies and decide them against using that analyst. Alternatively, these dire transference fantasies may throw them into panic. One such person became convinced (on the basis of a piece of art displayed in my consulting room) that I was about to commit suicide.

Even in infancy, caretakers can only provide an adequate holding environment if the newborn is constitutionally equipped to participate in such a symbiotic system. Excessively damaged personalities are seldom analyzable—but this very fact shows that analyzability is founded on the bedrock of positive transferences from the earliest phases of life.

Summary

Although the hermeneutics of analytic transactions cannot yield a scientific theory of mentation, it is clinically essential to offer analysands timely, accurate, and tactful transference interpretations whenever their ubiquitous propensity to misconstrue the present in terms of their past experiences obstructs the acquisition of improved adaptive skills. In other words, from a therapeutic viewpoint, sound psychoanalytic hermeneutics are essential, although they are not in themselves curative.

While transference-as-resistance must be dealt with via effective interpretive interventions, it should not be overlooked that other aspects of transference actually promote change by raising affective intensities, thereby learning and increasing affect tolerance. Moreover, even the basic trust that enables patients to commit themselves to treatment must be understood as a form of transference repetition.

Part II / The Biology of Mentation

CHAPTER FIVE

Personality Development and Psychopathology

Oedipal and Narcissistic Pathologies

As long as Freud and his early associates confined the use of psychoanalysis-as-treatment to "transference neuroses," they rightly concluded that the problem in these conditions consists of the inability to resolve intrapsychic conflicts. As Freud (1926) ultimately stated, such a dilemma may lead to one of three consequences: inhibition of activity, bodily symptoms with symbolic meaning, or seemingly inexplicable anxiety. In clinical practice, the unresolved conflicts were generally found to be those between sexual or aggressive impulses on the one hand and the dictates of conscience or the constraints of the sense of reality on the other.

I illustrate what the pioneering analysts had in mind with another vignette from the analysis featured in the last chapter: When this patient began to be aware of wishes to be close to me (a manifestation of father transference), she reported feeling guilty about excessive indulgence in sweets:

"I feel like a naughty child . . . The candy is a concrete substitute for the analysis. Eating was an activity about which everyone in my family felt comfortable."

"Quite a contrast with your conflict about reaching out for me. Why do you consider it so wrong?"

"I don't know. It *is* wrong . . . I don't want to find out why!"

We did find out—it had to do with the wish to displace my wife. These are the dynamics Freud named the Oedipus complex. At the time of this interchange, the forbidden impulses were inhibited. Their persistence was manifested in the "compromise formation" of self-indulgence in sweets: minor naughtiness through which she rationalized her otherwise puzzling guilt.

The pathology in such a situation consists of neither the sexual/aggressive wishes nor the prohibitions against them but of the unending failure to resolve the issue. As I tried to show in chapter 4, change does not follow insight. This particular patient long continued to punish herself in everyday life for her transferential impulses: "I've been making myself a beautiful silk dress, and Friday I burned a hole in it. It's obvious I was punishing myself. It had something to do with missing the analysis [over the weekend]." The curative step was not insight into the conflict or into its childhood roots but (1) acceptance of the absurdity of meting out real penalties for imaginary crimes and (2) mastery of her rage about the frustration of her wishes.

Beyond interpretation of hitherto unconscious mental contents, further therapeutic measures are generally necessary (Gedo 1993a). These interventions have to deal with those mental dispositions that led to sweeping the childhood conflict under the rug by rendering it unconscious. In this case, narcissistic rage about being thwarted only abated much later in the analysis, when the patient's illusions of omnipotence had been overcome. In the last chapter, I described how the analysand's unconscious grandiose fantasies emerged. Optimal disillusionment gradually followed, for in adulthood the patient's sense of reality overcame these "pathogenic beliefs" (Weiss et al. 1986). Her rage had been stoked by a sense of entitlement that stemmed from a developmental phase earlier than the oedipal manifestations first engaged in this analysis.

Clinical experiences of this kind made clear for me that most analysands suffered from a variety of maladaptations referable to several different phases of childhood development. Any failure to acquire the psychological skills usually learned at a given phase—a condition of apraxia (Gedo 1988)—impairs the child's ability to master the challenges of later developmental stages. It is even more of an obstacle to have come out of earlier phases with structured dispositions we may call *dyspraxic*, that is, to have learned patterns of behavior that are *prima facie* maladaptive.

The difference between these types of psychological defect can be discerned by the contrasting responses of the two patients described in chapter 4 to the possibility of being meaningfully influenced by the analysis. The one whose treatment was to prove successful made jokes about having been brainwashed, but she was content to assimilate new skills—"I am going to let whatever comes come"—and thus overcame a host of apraxic difficulties. The analysand who left treatment at the threshold of being thus affected could not learn from analysis because she experienced such external influence as a threat to her basic identity. This kind of dyspraxia constitutes a severe learning block, for basic mental operations are best acquired in the context of human transactions. Although we have no information about when this particular patient formed this maladaptive disposition, it is safe to assume that it was in the process of structuring her self-organization, in a phase of development that even precedes the realm of illusions (central to the pathology of the other analysand).

Expectable Personality Development

The variety of apraxic and dyspraxic deficits encountered in analytic work is limitless, but we need a rational classification of the circumstances in which they have their genesis if effective therapeutic approaches are to be devised. Such a schema must be based on a map of (more or less) expectable personality development. The crux of mapping "normal" development is a series of maturational sequences of maximally important functions such as cognition, communication, and affective control. Note that information about these biological capacities has to be sought in the work of cognate disciplines: cognitive science, semiotics, neurophysiology. (Ignorance of their results has led many psychoanalytic theorists into serious errors. Efforts to elaborate a theory of development from analytic clinical observations alone usually led to the portrayal of the normal infant as a "psychotic dwarf with a good prognosis," to quote an old psychiatric witticism.)

A biologically based schema of personality development should, therefore, parallel the expectable maturation of the central nervous system. We now know that the organization of the brain is itself decisively influenced by environmental vicissitudes, especially by the input of the caretakers (Schore 1994). Nonetheless, the major markers of that process are constitutionally determined. In terms of personality development, the significant phases in the maturation of neural control are the following:

— Phase I is characterized by the absence of cortical input; the infant gradually forms a map of self-in-the-world, initially probably in the cerebellum.
— Phase II is that of right hemispheric[1] prefrontal control; affective input begins to be added to the core of the organized self-representation.
— Phase III is characterized by predominance of the left cerebral

hemisphere; the self-organization is stabilized through replication of the self-schema as a map in the parietal cortex. Symbolic capacities become available.

— Phase IV begins when maturation (particularly of the corpus callosum) vastly increases interhemispheric integration, thereby bringing differing motives into conflict.

— Phase V is characterized by increasing regulation via the prefrontal cortex.

Maturation of functions such as cognition, affectivity, semiosis, and the regulation of behavior is the dependent concomitant of the progressive organization of the central nervous system. Hence "psychopathology" should always be understood as a matter of disordered brain processes.

CNS Dysfunction and Psychopathology

If these processes are grossly disrupted by tissue pathology or neurochemical disorders, acute and/or chronic brain syndromes may result. In many instances, however, such syndromes manifest themselves only by way of "psychological" symptoms—often starting with alterations in affectivity and behavioral integration. The following case should illustrate this contingency.

About a decade after terminating a lengthy and difficult but reasonably successful analysis, a middle-aged woman died of a brain tumor. About halfway through that decade she had sought a consultation about a minor professional setback; as I understood the situation, this resulted from a severe error in judgment on her part. Not long after this, she wrote me an angry letter in which she informed me that she was severely depressed due to some (unspecified) malfeasance on my part and that she would seek psychological assistance elsewhere. In the next several years, we occasionally ran into each other in public places; as time went on, she became less and less controlled in her behavior toward me, finally assaulting me verbally with·a rageful tirade.

It is, of course, impossible to determine when during this process her brain tumor began. Even had her grievances been justified (and I believe they were delusional), the progressive loss of control in terms of accepted social standards would betoken a deterioration in judgment that reflected the neuropathology. It is entirely possible that the faux pas about which she consulted me some five or six years before her death and the depression that soon followed were the first indications of a regression in neural control. At the same time, in other contexts, her behavior was probably better adapted because there she did not have to deal with the emotional intensity of a negative transference.

In clinical work, one encounters rare instances where acute regression to some primitive mode of organization involves the entire personality. Such contingencies are generally quickly reversible: patients return unimpaired to their customary activities immediately after sessions during which they may have regressed to altered states of consciousness, loss of sphincter control, or even seizures. In other cases, only a segment of the personality is affected and the analysand remains able to respond rationally to the analytic process. For instance, "I have a new symptom: for some days, I've had no appetite. When I was little, I was never hungry. It started when mother went to work, and I had to get my own food during the day, so I wouldn't bother to eat." In this circumstance, one aspect of the patient is an insightful adult while in another aspect she is reexperiencing the biological organization of a depressed child. This is the condition that in psychoanalytic discourse has usually been described as *splitting*.

Whether all or only part of the personality is implicated, behavioral integration always fluctuates among the modes of organization referable to the phases of neurological development the individual has traversed. In adulthood, the modes of all childhood phases continue to be available, although, in most circumstances, the most recently acquired mode supersedes earlier ones. In other words, a hierarchy of modes of functional organization is established in the course of development. Good adaptation implies the ability to employ all modes in a flexible manner, making use of whichever happens to yield best results in a given situation.[2]

More or less expectable development may be graphically portrayed as a model wherein time is represented in the horizontal dimension and overall maturation in the vertical. On such a diagram, the development of neural control and of its various dependent concomitants might be represented by diagonal arrows rising from left to right. The continuing availability of specific functional modes is indicated by the arrows within the model (fig. 5.1).

Developmental Disorders

One class of psychopathology is that of arrests of development, that is, failures in functional maturation in the realm of behavioral regulation. Individuals so affected are only able to meet the demands of adult existence by receiving reliable assistance from a symbiotic partner. Such needs for a symbiotic existence need not involve any impairment in cognition or semiosis, but in such cases affective regulation is usually poor. This kind of dependence on others almost always constitutes a severe injury to self-esteem that often leads to compensatory fantasies of grandiosity (see Kohut 1971). Consequently, such patients are often diagnosed as narcissistic personalities.

Any failure of the tenuous adaptation based on continuous availability of a symbiosis may lead to threatening states of helplessness and storms of dysphoric affect. Psychological contingencies of that kind may be dealt with by means of a variety of home remedies: delinquent enactments, drugs and/or alcohol, bulimia, sexual excesses or perversions, compulsive gambling, or endless obsessive-compulsive behaviors. If such measures fail to patch over the lack of symbiotic assistance, there may follow a further collapse of behavioral integration into panic, withdrawal, or traumatic states.[3] These conditions often necessitate the provision of a sheltered environment.[4]

In biologically predisposed individuals, a similar sequence of psychological events may serve as the precipitating stress that leads to psychotic decompensation, either into depressive (or manic) states or into some form of schizophrenia. In certain instances, these psychotic breaks are temporary but recurrent; in the past generation, patients with such a fluctuating course have often been termed *borderline*.

Another type of physiological predisposition leads, on the basis of nonspecific stresses, to the emergence of a variety of somatic disorders. In my clinical experience, migraine was the most frequent; I have also dealt with analogous instances of epilepsy, mucous colitis, bronchial asthma, and neurodermatitis. In all such cases, it should be possible to help patients to minimize these conditions by acknowledging the limits of their stress tolerance.

When, from a psychoanalytic perspective, the expectable development of behavior regulation has been arrested, this does not imply that there has been a complete arrest in the maturation of neural control. It does mean that the relevant synaptic networks are relatively sparse or, if you will, that there are widespread apraxic deficits. Such a state of affairs is found in many cases in which there is no overall arrest in the development of behavior regulation. Even less pervasive disturbances in development may lead to considerable adaptive disadvantages, albeit these may not entail the risks of decompensation described above.

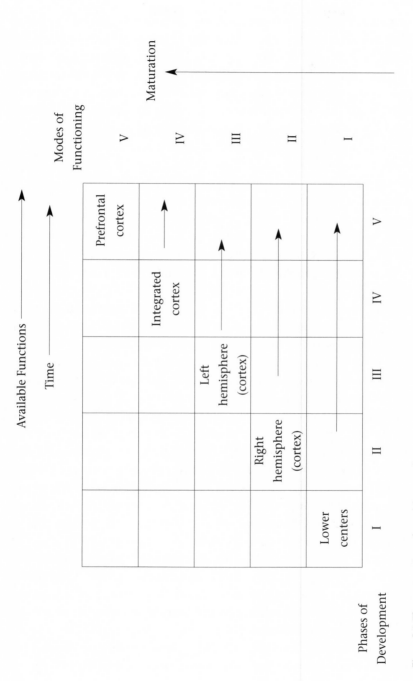

Figure 5.1. The maturation of neural control

As I have outlined in previous publications (Gedo 1988, 1993a), each of the principal developmental phases of early childhood presents the maturing individual with a number of challenges, among which, from the viewpoint of categorizing pathology, one may be singled out as characteristic of that phase. To take these in developmentally reverse order, the principal challenge while the input of the two cerebral hemispheres is being correlated (phase IV) is to develop the ability to reconcile their conflicting dispositions. (I began this chapter with a clinical vignette that illustrates a failure in this regard.) While (in phase III) the left hemisphere is gaining dominance, it is crucial to acquire the capacity to subject mental contents to rational consideration (reality testing), that is, to give up illusions. In the presymbolic world of phase II, with maturing affective controls (primarily in the right hemisphere), it is most important to develop a constant set of motivational priorities—what I have called the *self-organization* (Gedo 1979). The principal achievement to be accomplished in phase I, before there is significant cortical input, is effective tension regulation.

Relative failure to meet this sequence of challenges leads to a set of characteristic psychopathologies. As I have already mentioned, inability to resolve intrapsychic conflicts gives rise to the syndromes formerly called transference neuroses. When reality testing is faulty with regard to assessments of the child's own self or those of the caretakers, the resultant illusions yield the syndromes generally termed narcissistic. (As the illustration earlier in this chapter demonstrates, the same person may simultaneously suffer from both handicaps.) Failures to correlate various motivational subsets into a single hierarchy of goals produces "self-cohesion disturbances" (Gedo 1993a). The most familiar of these syndromes is one in which the patient is only aware of a "false self," while a "true self," potentially laden with suffering, remains unconscious. (The terms were introduced by Winnicott [1954]). As for phase I, less than optimal tension regulation renders the person vulnerable to traumatization and/or understimulated states of subjective emptiness.[5]

In parallel with figure 5.1, where the maturation of neural control is depicted, that of behavior regulation and its main pathological variants may be diagrammed, as in figure 5.2. The conditions that pertain to each phase and each mode of functioning available in that phase have been entered for each cell of the diagram in verbal form.

The maturational challenge of any phase of development may defeat a child because of contemporaneous environmental deprivations (such as severe somatic illness, the loss of a caretaker, or other traumatic events), but in most instances it is determined (or at least codetermined) by less than adequate resolution of the maturational tasks of previous developmental phases. (This developmental principle is valid in all of biology—it is termed the *epigenetic* view of development.) The etiology of such cumulative developmental failures generally involves the combination of atypical constitutional endowments and less than optimal nurture. The maturation of behavioral regulation is particularly likely to be impaired whenever there is maldevelopment in the realms of cognition and semiosis.[6]

Robbins (1987) has rightly pointed out that, in most cases, much of the analyst's therapeutic work consists of "cognitively oriented" interventions. Analysands have to be assisted to distinguish among thoughts, emotions, and actions; they have to be taught to reflect before they act; they need to learn to give priority to adaptively relevant issues; the analyst has to alert them to the importance of defensive behaviors, internal inconsistencies in thinking, the signal functions of bodily experience, and so on. These are only some of the apraxias in the cognitive and semiotic realms that predispose people to personality disorders.

The Role of Self-organization

An entirely different class of psychopathology, wherein development as such is not directly implicated, is the occurrence of compulsively repetitive behaviors with no apparent motive. As recounted in chapter 1, Freud (1920) rightly classified these phenomena to be "beyond the pleasure principle," for they are not performed for pleasure or profit—in fact, they persist even if they produce pain or loss. Freud postulated that such behaviors must satisfy some biological need, but the need he proposed (a form of inborn entropy or primary masochism) turned out not to be biologically valid. The problem was neglected for many years—as were most matters that pertain to the presymbolic universe (phases I and II).

It was only when theoreticians tackled the issue of "primary identity" (Lichtenstein 1961) that a better hypothesis emerged: certain behaviors have to be continually repeated to maintain the continuity of a sense of self. In my judgment, the latter is the subjective component of a map of "self-in-the-world" encoded in the brain (Levin 1991). Such a map is best conceptualized as a structured, unconscious "self-organization" (Gedo 1999). This consists of

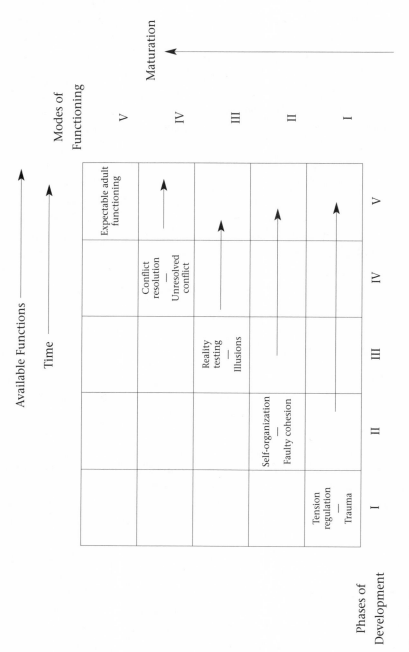

Figure 5.2. The maturation of behavior regulation and its characteristic pathologies

a system of memories that continues to guide behavior: whenever some action fails to echo anything in the self-system, the disjunction between present and past becomes conscious as a "not me" signal. The self-organization as a unitary structure that encompasses all organismic goals is generally complete before verbal competence is achieved. Thereafter, novel experiences may slowly alter the system—witness the effectiveness of many analytic efforts as well as their usual lengthy duration.

If in analysis we succeed in halting repetitive but obligatory enactments, patients almost always go through a period of bewilderment and depersonalization ("I am not me any more. Who am I, after all?")[7] The power of the repetition compulsion was brilliantly satirized in the motion picture *Doctor Strangelove*, whose protagonist is forever struggling to suppress the Nazi salute he automatically initiates.

The self-organization may also be involved in pathology if it is disrupted by circumstances that prevent too broad a range of its customary repetitions. Such contingencies may sometimes occur in the clinical situation; these analytic crises were first noted by Kohut (1971), who described them in terms of "fragmentation" of the sense of self. In biological terms, this amounts to a regression from more mature modes of organization to mode II, where the self-organization has not as yet been integrated—instead there are several nuclei of self that coexist without coordination. In analysis, such disruptions of self-cohesion tend to occur when, after the establishment of a transference-symbiosis, the analyst becomes temporarily unavailable. Adults experience this kind of regression with severe confusion, altered states of consciousness, and panic.

Summary

Clinical experience with a variety of syndromes gradually revealed that psychopathology is best understood in terms of developmental considerations, for each developmental phase (defined as a mode of organization of the central nervous system) corresponds to a distinct cluster of apraxic and dyspraxic possibilities, whenever its challenges are poorly met. The hierarchical arrangement of the central nervous system leads to the possibility that behavior regulation may be arrested at primitive levels, in whole or (in the case of splitting) in part. Such arrests predispose affected individuals to a variety of severe biological sequelae, depending on constitutional vulnerabilities.

The major exception to the developmental origin of psychopathology is the occurrence of inconvenient repetitive behaviors as obligatory manifestations of a need to ensure the continuity of the basic self-organization consolidated in the presymbolic era of existence. Even this exception, however, is referable to the disposition of biological variables. In other words, the whole issue of psychopathology is optimally conceptualized in such biological terms.

CHAPTER SIX

A Hierarchy of Motivations as Self-organization

Psychoanalysis claims to be depth psychology par excellence because it goes beyond the study of human wishes in conflict to postulate a set of underlying preverbal motivations. According to dictionaries, *motivation* refers to whatever impels a person to act—or, in more restrictive versions, to act volitionally. In Freud's (1900) metapsychology, the focus shifted to mental acts, and motivation became the force that sets the mental apparatus in motion and can be viewed from a "dynamic" viewpoint. This metaphoric conceptualization presented depth psychology in the language of physics, particularly of the study of electricity. Just as electricity is viewed simultaneously in terms of volts, ohms, and amperes, Freud made use of motivational concepts of forces, resistances, and energies. Thus the notion of dynamics implicitly required complementary concepts of inhibiting structure and of intensities. Freud outlined such a theoretical schema between 1892 and 1900.

Thereafter, Freud tried to define the nature of psychological forces in terms of innate, constitutionally determined biological potentialities he called *Trieben.* At first he subdivided these into "self-preservative" and sexual motives; because this classification failed to account for narcissistic issues, libidinal drives were further differentiated (Freud 1914b) into narcissistic and object libido. Discovery of various automatic repetitions of behavior (such as those observed in traumatic neuroses during the World War I) again showed the inadequacy of this classificatory scheme. In 1920, Freud therefore proposed his ultimate theory of motivation, in which he counterposed life and death "instincts." This proposal required no basic change in the underlying biological assumptions Freud had used for three decades.

The majority of analytic theoreticians have refused to accept the concept of a death instinct and have also abandoned Freud's attempt to articulate an inclusive theory of motivation. This is true of those who have adopted Heinz Hartmann's proposal (1939) of a dual drive theory of libidinal and aggressive motivations. That schema leaves out all motives that Freud initially called "self-preservative," as well as those underlying the behavioral phenomena he attributed to a "repetition compulsion." Hartmann's heirs (the school called ego psychology) have also failed to note that if the assumption that drive theory must apply to the entire range of motivated behaviors is abandoned, it is no longer necessary to accept Freud's a priori postulate that narcissistic motivations are fueled by libido. For the past generation or so, psychoanalysis has not had a coherent theory of motivation.

Lichtenberg (1989) made a fresh start with an effort to classify those universal human goals that presumably have constitutional roots. He posits five independent preprogrammed biological patterns of motivation: attachment, aversion, active exploration, sensuality/sexuality, and the maintenance of physiological equilibria. In 1989, Hadley reviewed the relevant neurophysiological data then available; she confirmed that structures mediating behaviors serving the aims listed by Lichtenberg do exist in the brain. Because neural structures subserving further organismic goals may be found, additional preprogrammed motivations may have to be added to such a list. In 1992, Hadley reported that the biological evidence compels the separation of sexual from sensual motivations, thereby expanding the list of preprogrammed patterns to six. Nonetheless, Lichtenberg's schema takes cognizance of "self-preservative" aims, as well as sexual and aggressive ones.

Whether or not Lichtenberg's theory of motivation is adequately inclusive, it has abandoned the matrix of Freud's metapsychology. Lichtenberg's motivational systems are not conceived as drives pressing for discharge or as forces bound to encounter structural resistance and characterized by measurable intensities. Thus his theory is not an extrapolation from the physics of an electrical apparatus; rather, it is an application of cybernetics. As such, it relies on a contemporary understanding of the operations of neural control rather than on the brain science and biological models of the 1890s.

Preprogrammed biological patterns are uninterruptedly available; each is evoked by the adaptive requirements for which it is appropriate. Thus sexual or aggressive motives come into play in response to specific stimuli, not because of built-up drive pressures. When fantasy activity becomes possible, sexual (or aggressive) responses can be stimulated endogenously without external cues.[1] Insofar as sexuality does operate in accord with a preprogrammed "blueprint," this simple program can only prevail before being integrated into more complex hierarchies of motivation.

Freed of the constraints of equating motivation with *Trieben*, we may extend its definition beyond the realm of the preprogrammed patterns essential for survival. Complex human priorities cannot be determined solely by preprogrammed patterns wired into the brain. These considerations impelled Freud to postulate "narcissistic libido"—a desperate conceptual tour de force designed to extend drive psychology into realms lacking direct connections to our presymbolic world. Mentation involving abstractions such as good and bad constitutes a universe much more complex than do inborn patterns of organismic response—whether we view such inborn programs as drives or as cybernetic arrangements. This is not to say that human ideals are disembodied but that, with regard to such "higher" functions (in 1923, Freud called them "super-ego"), what is built into the nervous system is the capacity to regulate behavior on the basis of manipulating abstract symbols.

Perhaps it is best to differentiate motivations preprogrammed to subserve adaptation from the power of abstract ideas to propel human behavior. Moreover, it must be kept in mind that every piece of behavior simultaneously serves several purposes (Waelder 1930). It is entirely possible to aspire to an aristocracy of virtue in order to fulfill some aversive goal—for example, to distance oneself from a despised parent—while, at the same time, this ambition satisfies a wish for moral excellence. Hence it is preferable to approach complex matters of this kind through a hierarchical schema (Wilson and Gedo 1993).

Insofar as inborn programs for action are present from birth, the simplest and most basic system of human motivations is in force only so long as these biological potentialities operate in pure culture, unmodified by actual experience. (These are the conditions we may call mode I in a hierarchical schema of motivations.) The influence of experience makes itself felt by means of remembered patterns of affective responses typically evoked by various contingencies, especially patterns of pleasure and pain. Pleasure, pain, and other affects are preprogrammed organismic responses to specific kinds of events within the nervous system. (The realm of affects is elaborated in chapter 9.) Yet *memories* of previously experienced sensations may serve as signals about the expectable consequences of various behaviors. Whenever a system of such signals becomes operative, the organism has acquired a second order of motivations—what Freud variously termed the pleasure principle or that of *unpleasure*. *Unpleasure* is more appropriate, for the threat of unpleasant feelings is most likely to override other motivations. When organismic motivations are supplemented by the guidance of memory-signals, conditions may be classified as a more differentiated mode (mode II).

Insofar as behavior becomes guided by the principle of avoiding unpleasure, the resultant activities will *on the surface* appear to be aversive; that is, they will seem to be motivated in terms of the preprogrammed schemata of "aversion." It is true that these functions will be recruited to effect the necessary actions, but *at bottom* the resultant behavior is determined by a constitutional preference for one affective state over another. The neonate may look for novelty because exploratory schemata are wired into the brain, but soon the infant will engage in exploratory behaviors because they were previously pleasurable (or avoid them because they were not). Such a change corresponds to the progressive organization of the central nervous system for ever more complex functioning: a neurophysiological subsystem "which supplies both positive and negative motivations depending on the outcomes of the matching process and the addition of affect" is activated in the course of development (Hadley 1989, 337).

The need to keep the intensity of affects within prescribed boundaries and to promote the occurrence of preferred emotional experiences (and to avoid those for which there is aversion) has been widely understood. Putting these desiderata in protophysiological terms links the theory I propose with Stern's (1985) emphasis on the crucial role, *prior* to the attainment of symbolic capacities, of affective attunement between child and mother. (This matter is further elaborated in Fonagy et al. 2002.) The quantitative and qualitative parameters of the affective patterns then established in a privileged position form the core of experience that human beings are compelled to repeat, at any cost, to maintain the continuity of their self-organization (see Gedo 1979, 1993a, and this book, chap. 5).

It is never self-evident whether any specific activity will evoke pleasure or unpleasure, even if, taken in isolation, its effects are uniform. In other words, no activity occurs in isolation but only in the context of complex transactions with the milieu. Thus infants with unusual experiences may learn that exploratory behavior is followed by very unpleasant consequences—or that temporary spells of unpleasure are rewarded by long-term satisfaction. Whenever an individual is consistently subjected to such paradoxical results, the system of affective signals will produce seemingly maladaptive motivations, capable of overriding "expectable" motivational schemata. Such behavioral dispositions are usually called *masochistic.* The first analysand described in chapter 4 exemplifies this pattern: she arranged to live in masochistic bondage until, after years of effort, her analysis impelled her to break free. At that juncture, she began to feel that the analysis would infringe on her personal autonomy, and she discontinued treatment. In other words, to lead a conventionally "healthy" life promised, in her long-term experience, less satisfaction than did continuing submission to a tyrant. Even such choices are matters of taste! The analyst was not tyrannical enough to qualify as a sadistic partner.

The evolution of motivational complexity does not stop with the acquisition of the foregoing second layer of causation for behavior. Repetition of patterns of affectomotor activity will relatively quickly result in the formation of a model of self-in-the-world. Repetitions of behavior are measured by comparator mechanisms that signal their attainment by means of neurochemical changes that produce subjective "satisfactions" (Hadley 1989). These are the neural functions corresponding to the phenomena psychoanalysis has attributed to the repetition compulsion. When self-organization has become stable, the rate of tolerable change is so reduced that the need to maintain it within the boundaries of comfort becomes a third type of motivating force for human behavior. These are the conditions of mode III in a hierarchical model of motivations.

The need to preserve the integrity of self-organization is a biological imperative—that is why the repetition compulsion overrides all matters simply concerned with pleasure and profit. In contrast to its ceaseless pressure, pre-programmed schemata are engaged on an ad hoc basis. As rational and social considerations gradually gain more influence on behavioral choices, even the operation of the pleasure/unpleasure principle becomes merely episodic. Hence the formation of a stable self-organization is equivalent to the integration into a single hierarchy of aims of the disparate biologically determined motivations of the infant. Henceforth the maintenance of this macrostructure assumes a supraordinate role for the individual.

This enduring state of affairs is then greatly complicated by the transformation of the child from an organism regulated via biological automatisms and by affectomotor cues from the caretaker to a being capable of symbolic operations. These cognitive gains enable the child to grasp whatever increases or decreases its value in the estimation of the parents and to accept the standards implicit in such judgments. At this stage, children also become capable of learning a system of symbols for the affects; as a result, they are enabled to achieve emotional self-awareness.

It is true that, as early as the end of the first year of life, infants experience joy or shame, depending on the mother's (primary caretaker's) facial expression. Affective responses to the latter's smile or frown are automatic: the infant cannot judge as good or bad its behavior that elicited approval or disapproval (Schore 1994). It is the fact that joy gives pleasure and shame produces unpleasure that gives caretakers the power to control the child's behavior. Self-awareness is only achieved toward the end of the second year of life, in parallel with the acquisition of verbal communication. Even then, it is necessary for such progress that caretakers connect various verbal symbols of *good* and *bad* with the actions of which they approve or disapprove. Henceforth, verbal transactions are mediated by responses along a pride/shame axis. A new pathway for motivating behavior becomes available, that of pleasure/unpleasure in response to conceptual categories, which initiates the fourth phase in the development of the motivational hierarchy.

This development ushers in the ability to experience intrapsychic conflict about a wish, as the child learns simultaneously to keep in mind symbolically encoded memories of incompatible wishes. The need to avoid painful affects then gives rise to disavowal or repression. The power to forestall unpleasure through these defensive operations greatly increases the ability to pursue most of the child's organismic goals—at the price of frustrating certain wishes. (The issue of defensive operations is discussed in detail in chapter 8). Before this phase, children are unable, when left to their own devices, to maintain behavioral integration; caretakers have to establish priorities on their behalf. Henceforth, as creatures of self-awareness, children are able to establish priorities among their wishes on the basis of the remembered affective consequences of their fulfillment or frustration.

Clinical experience has taught us that shame may be insufficient to override motivations stemming from the need to maintain the stability of the self-organization—most clearly in instances where stability requires some symptomatic behavior that induces shame but is endlessly repeated nonetheless. If, however, early conflict between ideals and stability arises in a particularly intense and prolonged manner, this potentially traumatic circumstance often leads to defensive splitting and a permanent division of the personality into disparate "nuclei" (see Gedo and Goldberg 1973).

The importance of self-organization and its disruption into uncorrelated segments can be illustrated by describing the termination phase of the analysis I described in previous chapters. The patient realized that her treatment was approaching its end when she took a vacation without discussing the matter with me in advance. While she was away, she managed very well; on her return, she had a nightmare about an accident in which her leg was severed. This was the first indication, after three years of analysis, that in the mother transference she experienced a fantasied merger with me—she was entirely clear that the dream was about impending loss of the analysis.[2]

Shortly thereafter, during an analytic session, she experienced what had been a repetitive symptom through her early years: "The sensation is so real— I am here and I'm not. Unusual things are happening to my body, as if there were cylinders turning, like watchworks. I fit into the middle of this—only my head is outside. It's a feeling of anxious excitement and, at the same time, depression—it fills me with nausea and pain. Inside I'm all numb; all my sensation is on the skin surface, as if I didn't exist otherwise: like a vacuum inside."[3]

This is highly trained self-observation by a sophisticated adult (one who is functioning in mode V); simultaneously, her subjective experience is the emergence of a wordless state in which the sense of self is barely preserved as a container of severe dysphoria. For the first time in the analysis, the distress of the true self is fully acknowledged.

Modell's (1992) cogent suggestion that such split-off islands of experience are best conceived as the "private self" was highlighted by a dream my analysand reported in the very same session. This concerned giving away her overcoat. "A coat keeps one protected and covered . . . In a sense, it keeps one invisible. In the dream, it refers to my facade, to all the defenses I had before analysis." She was ready to uncover her private self.

For the following few weeks, the patient revealed an inner core that operated at the level of a two year old. This was fraught with feelings of helplessness and anxiety; outside her sessions, however, she felt more self-confident than ever. She was having dreams about desiring the death of maternal figures; she connected these with her life-long rage at her mother. She began to feel unprecedented levels of anger at me, like the breath-holding tantrums she remembered having had in early childhood. She knew that her rage was about the power of mothers and analysts to abandon her.

In some sessions, she babbled like an infant on the verge of acquiring verbal language. In this context she had a dream that revealed the roots of her life-long masochism:

I was a prisoner in a forest, miles from everyone—no, there were two of us. Our captors were very cruel; they cut our soles with razor blades . . . I thought of crawling away, and right away they skinned my hands and knees. Whatever escape I devised, they immediately mutilated the relevant part of my body! I was apparently free, but it was impossible to get away. This was a dream of self-torture; it expressed my masochism. I wonder who was with me? This person lent me comfort and courage; we were on a common mission. We would never get away from each other.

The dream portrayed the self-damaging behaviors through which she had always attempted to bind caretakers to herself by compelling them to lend comfort to an inconsolable being. She seemed to have crystallized this resolution before the acquisition of language. For some time, I failed to realize that she often succeeded in making me feel like an inadequate caretaker through wordless enactments—in the countertransference, I was irritated by her endless suffering. The patient overcame this repetition of the past by connecting her straying into this blind alley with events she had all along known about: when she was barely two years old, her mother was hospitalized for several months with a life-threatening illness. The patient had been unable to reconsider her reactions in that crisis, for these had never registered as verbal memories; they were unrememberable but unforgettable (Frank 1969) as affecto-motor dispositions. The reconsideration that now took place integrated the split-off segment of the self-organization into the patient's adult organization. This is the process I prefer to call *unification* (Gedo and Goldberg 1973).

The curative step within this process was mastery of the patient's need to have complete control of her relationships. Unless she was master, she felt cruelly robbed of her volition, and she treated her slaves with arrogance and cruelty:

"I know that you are at my mercy, like the dentist when I was a child. I would bite him as he was working . . . They were helpless against my opposition."

She then realized that she had been equally negativistic throughout the analysis.

"I feel terrible—I cheated myself and I have cheated you."
"Yes, you cheat me of the fruits of my labor, because I will not consent to be at one with you, on your terms."
"It was like that with mother."

This exchange showed that she was now conscientiously disapproving of behaviors that had previously been processed in mode II, without internalized controls.

Are we justified in classifying motives that arise as a result of the onset of shame and pride (or, at a somewhat later stage, the analogous operation of guilt) as independent sources of behavioral initiative? French (1952) suggested that we call these "acquired" reasons for human action "countermotives" to indicate that these motivations arise as a consequence of superego formation. This achievement signifies that the child has learned to approve or disapprove his or her own behaviors. Felicitous development requires a self-organization flexible enough in terms of rate of change to assimilate the countermotives learned from the caretakers without inducing defensive splitting. With such accommodation, superego standards become hierarchically dominant, and the four classes of motivation thus far discussed are smoothly integrated into one assembly. This development constitutes the single most drastic change in self-organization in the life cycle.

If the motivations acquired during this fourth phase of development represent the functional entity Freud named *superego,* those added in the course of later life are the motives for action related to the functions Hartmann (1939) conceptualized as the aspects of "ego" subserving optimal adaptation. The voice of reason and "common sense" gradually gains influence on behavior as the individual becomes less dependent on caretakers to monitor decisions. Hence the timing of the acquisition of these motivations is widely variable: some children learn to rely on their own judgment as early as the age of eight to ten; most people seem to assume these burdens in adolescence; still others only do so sometime in adult life—or never.

I conclude that adequate development implies the integration of motives stemming from the following sources:

1. inborn preprogrammed motivations
2. the differentiation of the pleasure/unpleasure gradient
3. the overarching importance of a stable self-organization
4. the internalization of ideals (and imperatives)
5. the learned requirements of adequate adaptation

This modal progression is represented graphically in figure 6.1.

Summary

In psychoanalysis, motivation has always been conceptualized in biological terms, but only recently has this conceptualization been correlated with the

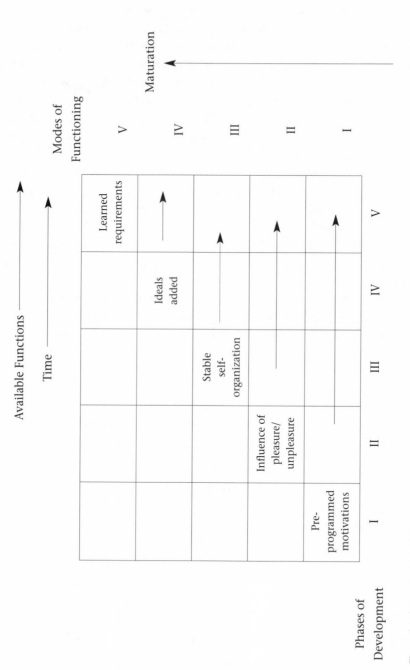

Figure 6.1. A motivational hierarchy

phasic development of the central nervous system. Each of these successive phases introduces greater complexity into the hierarchy of motivations (as figure 6.1 illustrates).

Basic self-organization can be understood as the stable structuralization of preferred subjective experiential patterns encompassing all the inborn organismic motivations and their affective concomitants. Changes in this presymbolic, unconscious macrostructure can later occur, but only slowly and gradually. In other words, the need to maintain stability in self-organization in itself becomes a motivational imperative.

CHAPTER SEVEN

Trauma and Its Vicissitudes

Disruption of Self-organization

One neuropsychiatric concept in continuous use throughout the history of psychoanalysis has been that of *trauma*. The notion was current in late-nineteenth-century medical discourse; Freud took it over from his most influential mentor, the Parisian neurologist Jean Martin Charcot (Miller et al. 1969). Although it has been customary to broaden the definition of trauma to encompass exposure to almost any unpleasant stimulus, watering down the concept so that trauma and stress are equated robs it of significance. For psychoanalytic purposes, the most useful definition is a narrow one. In accord with such a definition, to qualify as an actual trauma, an event must have certain definite phenomenological consequences.

Trauma as Disorganization

Greenacre's excellent description of a traumatic outcome was quoted in chapter 2. She emphasized the simultaneous emergence of confusion, changes in consciousness, severe anxiety and/or rage, and various vegetative symptoms. In "posttraumatic disorders," this syndrome recurs repetitively—an outcome already described in cases of "shell shock" during World War I (Abraham et al. 1919). This kind of reliving is particularly apt to occur in the form of anxiety dreams, but it can also emerge in the context of the analysis of personality disorders based on early traumatic experiences, against the repetition of which more or less successful defenses have been effected. (In such instances, reliving the original traumas in the treatment denotes the relaxation of defensive vigilance in the service of attempted mastery.)

I can best illustrate this sequence of events through the case of a young professional woman who had been unable to provide a coherent history of her childhood.[1] Early in the treatment, she had frequent dissociative episodes during her sessions—she called these "flipping out." She blamed me for precipitating these, as it turned out, correctly: we eventually found that she had been unable to integrate the analytic experiences that might be summed up as an ambience of empathic acceptance. In childhood, her mother and an older sister consistently brainwashed her (via grossly fictive assertions of what had transpired between them). Within the transference, my attempted helpfulness was therefore initially misconstrued as threatening entrapment; interpretation of such misjudgments left her utterly bewildered. None of the programs of action within her repertory were applicable to her novel circumstances.

In the course of a lengthy analysis, it came to light that this person had managed to achieve outward success by means of a false self devoid of affectivity. Her true self was split off and disavowed. This tenuous adaptation could be maintained only through minimizing meaningful human contacts; such schizoid withdrawal became almost impossible in a psychoanalytic context. This analysand was unable to cope with the novelty of a nonabusive relationship that encouraged the emergence of the true self and of the compulsive repetition of sadomasochistic transactions. These continued to characterize the analytic process for years once the patient was able to assimilate pain-filled experiences as her own. "Flipping out" had been the regressive avoidance of this imperative need for chronic suffering, retreat to a primitive mode of organization lacking in language and full consciousness. In other words, the novel experience in analysis disrupted her self-organization; "traumatization" consisted of falling back on the repertory of mode I.

In the past, traumatic events were attributed to an accumulation of tension, either through overstimulation or because the discharge of excitation has been blocked. (Freud [1894, 1898] postulated that when sexual satisfaction is impeded, the result is increased tension and organismic disequilibrium in the form of anxiety that is without psychological meaning.) In my clinical experience, mounting levels of tension are generally successfully aborted because susceptible individuals guard against reexperiencing traumatic disruptions. If such defensive efforts are unsuccessful, the immediate sequelae are not trauma but increased irritability, hyperacuity in various sensory modalities, photophobia, paraesthesias, restlessness, and insomnia.

Alternatively, just the threat of a disruption of the self-organization may produce severe anxiety. Hence the "anxiety neuroses" without psychological significance Freud observed early in his career may have been syndromes that denoted threats to self-cohesion. Traumatic disruptions are, however, likely to occur only in predisposed individuals—those who underwent repeated traumas early in life—for instance, repeated incidents of sexual abuse. These may well have been overstimulating, but they most likely resulted in traumas be-cause the child could not categorize the behavior of its abuser in terms of its previous experience. The analysand who "flipped out" when I subjected her to unfamiliar experiences had that kind of childhood history; this person was never traumatized, even by transactions of maximal affective intensity, as long as these experiences were familiar to her from the past.

It is also true that regression to the earliest mode of functional organization makes an individual extremely vulnerable both to overstimulation and to stim-ulus deprivation. These findings led me to conclude that, from a clinical per-spective, the greatest challenge the infant must overcome in phase I of devel-opment is that of effective tension regulation (Gedo and Goldberg 1973). Those persons who fail to learn how to manage their transactions with their milieu so that they will experience neither too little nor too much stimula-tion may undergo drastic physiological changes whenever there are major quantitative shifts in levels of stimulation, whether the stimuli come from the outside (as in the war neuroses) or from within. These are the susceptible in-dividuals who may respond to overstimulation with loss of consciousness and/or sphincter control, uncoordinated spasms, profuse sweating, even seizures. Instances of this kind have led to the metaphoric characterization of traumatization as an explosive disintegration.

Trauma and Mentalist Theories

Whatever theoretical differences there are among various conceptualiza-tions of trauma, there is no disagreement that it is a neurophysiological phe-nomenon. Hence theoreticians who claim that they use only psychological concepts cannot legitimately employ that of trauma; to do so in a mentalist context is to be guilty of incoherence. Mentalists whose theories are internally consistent tend altogether to avoid the subject of trauma. For example, in Kohut's Self Psychology, this concept of neurophysiological disorganization has been replaced by the notion of subjective "fragmentation." No doubt such a sense of internal disarray overlaps with the objective notion of disorganiza-tion, but not entirely so; analysands may feel "fragmented" without having lost self-cohesion. Witness the profound regressive experience in the analytic situation of the patient described in chapter 4: she felt as if she had been an as-sembly of mechanical parts, but she was also continuously aware of the bound-aries of her being. Purely phenomenological theories, such as that of Kohut

(Modell 1992), rely excessively on the unreliable subjectivity of their subjects. To give credit where it is due, Kohut at least describes deeply regressive events that may involve disorganization. In contrast, a "relational theorist" such as Mitchell (1988) does not even mention these issues—only psychological processes that involve a relationship matter—and a radical hermeneuticist such as Schafer (1976) explicitly denies any possibility that human experiences could be nonvolitional.

In 1926 Freud put forward a theory of neurosogenesis that relied on the idea that it is the danger of traumatization that impels the individual to abort intensifying anxiety by means of inhibition or symptom formation. This was acknowledgment of the ever-present potentiality of overstimulation from within. As I mentioned in chapter 1, Freud neglected to specify the physiological mechanism of trauma; nonetheless, his hypothesis that the earliest emergence of anxiety acts as a signal to put defensive operations in motion constituted the abandonment of a power-engineering model of mind, based on concepts of forces and energies, in favor of a cybernetic one.

Within psychoanalysis, the importance of trauma was next emphasized by Balint (1932). He reduced all psychopathology to a sequel of trauma, and he proposed that it could be overcome through the provision of a positive relationship. (More recently, Kohut [1984] and his school expressed a very similar idea as the provision of an empathic ambience.) Balint's prescription adopted the latest views of Ferenczi (1928, 1931), which almost entirely focused on therapeutics. The so-called "object relations theorists" who succeeded them gradually drifted into the mentalist position exemplified by Mitchell. Theorists who espouse the notion that a benign new relationship will promote maturation through a "new beginning" (as Balint put it) are making an assumption about human biology and cannot claim adherence to purely hermeneutic/mentalist premises.

Personality Disorders Based on Trauma

I have previously stated (Gedo 1996, chap. 9) that the Ferenczi-Balint prescription may be effective in cases of developmental arrest uncomplicated by structured dyspraxias. Both Anna Freud (1965) and Winnicott (1965) stressed that "unhitching a developmental catch" in children is often feasible through the provision of a "new and different emotional experience." In my judgment, such simple measures are seldom successful with adults because childhood traumas are almost always followed by unfavorable characterological developments. In analysis, such patients produce transferences that repeat childhood patterns of behavior, designed to deal with the consequences of trauma, that turn out to be maladaptive in later life. Relying on the analytic relationship alone to cure such problems usually leads to interminable analyses. As Bruno Bettelheim (1950) kept reiterating, "Love is not enough."

I can illustrate the impossibility of promoting a "new beginning" in these cases through an example presented to me in a seminar.[2] The patient was an accomplished professional woman who sought help because of problems with intimacy. She was so terrified of reliving her early childhood traumas that through a long period of the treatment she withdrew into somnolence. It took several years of analytic work to reach a clear understanding that this was the crucial technical problem to overcome in the treatment. At the start of the analysis, the patient's behavior was utterly confusing: she insisted, with the utmost vehemence, that the analyst must condemn people who retaliated when she aggressively provoked them, without examining the patient's responsibility for the problem. It took the better part of a year to get past this seemingly paranoid attitude.

As it turned out, the analysand was enacting some of the scenarios that had traumatized her in childhood: the analyst was assigned the role of the patient-as-victim of her mother's crazy denials of her own responsibility for any derailment of their relationship. In other words, the traumatic past had been covered over through identification with the aggressor who caused the damage. Whatever new relationship the patient was offered, she forestalled any positive developments either through ceaseless efforts to provoke the other, even the analyst, or through turning away and falling asleep. A new beginning for her was contingent on reexperiencing her childhood traumas and gaining the skill to manage the transactions she had been unable to master as a child.

As Modell (1990) explained, analysis must provide the opportunity to retranscribe traumatic past experiences (that is, affect-laden memories) so that they acquire new meanings. For the patient just described, improvement was contingent on leaving behind her mother's senseless focus on blaming someone for life's difficulties; she needed to learn that it is possible to avoid being scapegoated without turning into a persecutor. Modell postulates that the setting of analysis (the physical environment, the schedule, financial arrangements—I would add the analyst's professionalism to his list) constitutes an environment of safety that facilitates reexperiencing the past even in its dreaded aspects. In agreement with Winnicott (1960), Modell calls such circumstances a "holding environment." Within this potential space, the participants can work to establish a shared reality.

Once this has been achieved, previously traumatic situations are mastered through repetition and recontextualization. Modell rightly states that such repetition involves a mosaic of affect categories; hence mastery amounts to affective retraining—the repair of a biological deficit. Another way to conceptualize the nature of the required change is that purely procedural memories have to be transformed into semantic ones—this is the "retranscription" Modell refers to. At the beginning of the foregoing analysis, the patient remembered the past only by reproducing it in action, with roles reversed, so that it was the analyst who experienced the affects of someone who was being driven crazy. In midtreatment, her memories of the same childhood transactions were encoded in verbal form. This shift denoted a small but crucial change in the organization of the brain.

Trauma and Stimulation

Holt (1989) looks upon trauma as disorganization of behavioral control as a result of informational overload—a purely quantitative explanation. This definition confines trauma to instances in which only mode I in the functional hierarchy is implicated, in contrast to my proposal that trauma involves disruption of the self-cohesion achieved in the next phase of development. It is true, of course, that overstimulation leads to traumatic disruption of self-cohesion; to maintain the maturational achievements of later phases, the functions of mode I must remain intact. It is even more important to keep in mind that lack of stimulation can also be traumatic, particularly so in early childhood. This finding can only mean that the self-organization is perpetuated not only through the repetition of behaviors that bring about familiar subjective experiences but also by way of familiar external perceptions.

In adult life, understimulated states occur extremely rarely, for almost everyone has the capacity to seek out whatever kind and level of stimulation is needed. In analysis, they do occur, however, as repetitions of unremembered past events of dire significance in individuals who suffered such deprivation as children. The following case summary illustrates this syndrome.[3]

A patient undertook treatment with me when a previous analysis reached an impasse. Almost immediately, he demonstrated a pattern of starting the week in his Monday sessions in a state approaching inertia: his thoughts came to him with excruciating slowness, and he could scarcely force himself to articulate them. He was preoccupied with his headache, dripping sinuses, and his constipation; he felt weak and cold; his extremities were numb; his fingers were visibly blue, and he was depersonalized. For years, he had ended up in this condition every weekend; it set in by Saturday afternoon and lifted during the day on Monday. His internist insisted the syndrome did not have a somatic etiology.

This man invariably spent the weekend entirely in solitude, depressed and full of self-pity. He tried to ward off the onset of the syndrome through physical exercise,[4] but he was gradually enveloped in weakness and somnolence, and he retreated into bed. Although these conditions abated if he was invited out, the patient never initiated social contacts. When he was confronted with these facts, he reluctantly planned his weekends so as to avoid solitude, whereupon he began to experience a variety of dysphoric reactions about my undue influence on him, while his puzzling physiological symptoms disappeared.

The patient's passive acceptance of the helplessness that overtook him "when all alone [he bewept his] outcast state" was an iatrogenically induced syndrome that reproduced infantile states induced by abandonment. In that sense, it was a set of procedural memories encoded as affectomotor acts. Indeed, when this man was born his mother suffered a severe postpartum depression from which she never fully recovered, so it is highly probable that he was grossly understimulated during infancy. He was ever vulnerable to lapsing into a state of emptiness and depression that undermined self-cohesion (depersonalization), thus leading to trauma.

Some Consequences of Trauma in Early Childhood

As several of the clinical vignettes in this chapter illustrate, persons who were subjected to trauma in early childhood never recall those events as semantic memories, but they have the potential to repeat the relevant transactions as affectomotor acts. That is why Frank (1969) called these events simultaneously unrememberable and unforgettable. Freud (1915c) referred to matters that never gained verbal encoding as "primarily repressed" (in contrast to semantic memories that are later barred from consciousness). Hadley reports that "when stimulus strength and arousal reach sufficient intensity, the hippocampal system shuts down . . . and only 'emotional memory' is laid down" (2000).

Children who suffer repeated early traumas and therefore react with much dysphoric affect may split off this nucleus of true self, as the cases cited also demonstrate. The child's emotional wounds are disavowed, and this permits maturation of most functions that will constitute an affectless false self.

The changes in consciousness that generally take place in the course of traumatization are adaptive somatic responses that interrupt dangerous peaks of affective intensity. Unceasing panic can potentially damage midbrain areas (the hippocampus) through the direct effect on nerve cells of excessive concentrations of neurochemicals (Levin and Trevarthen 2000). This destructive process is mitigated if lack of consciousness is accompanied by diminution of affect. Nonetheless, traumatic experiences may damage the very structures of affective control.

Summary

Trauma, a neuropsychiatric concept devised before the advent of psychoanalysis, refers to an observable biological syndrome in response to events that overwhelm the organism. In line with Freud's metapsychology, these were assumed to cause overstimulation; the traumatic consequences were described via metaphors that suggest an explosion. Alternatively, it has been proposed that the syndrome is caused by an information overload. There is, however, no empirical evidence for this suggestion.

Trauma is best conceptualized as a response to helplessness in the face of unfamiliar contingencies by way of temporary regression to the earliest mode of behavioral (and neural) organization. The loss of consciousness this entails serves to interrupt mounting panic. Neuropsychological events of this kind are inexplicable by way of mentalist theories.

CHAPTER EIGHT

Breakdowns in Information Processing

Some twenty-five years after he founded the discipline, Freud declared that a therapist who takes transference and resistance into account is doing psychoanalysis.[1] By resistance to therapeutic efforts he meant repression—for many years, the terms were used interchangeably. After 1927, when Freud differentiated the mental process he called disavowal from that of repression, it became necessary to confine the concept of resistance to the theory of therapeutics; for the various mental operations that subserve resistance, the term *defense* came into general use. In 1936, Anna Freud made a first attempt to describe a wide array of *defense mechanisms;* she conceived these as operations of the structure named *ego,* the primary function of which was postulated to be control over the untamed drives of the *id* (S. Freud 1923).

Repression

Although as early as 1895 (Breuer and Freud, chap. 4) repression was a key concept in Freud's theories, it was not until later (1915c) that he discussed it in detail as the exclusion of some verbally encoded mental content from consciousness, lest it cause unpleasure. Because his conception of mind depended on power engineering analogies, Freud had to explain the mechanism of repression as a process of draining an impulse of its energy; he was unable satisfactorily to account for the manner in which such an outcome might be achieved. As discussed in chapter 1, Freud's energetic hypotheses have been invalidated, so even his sketchy explanation of the mechanism of repression now has to be abandoned.

As a clinical observation, however, the operation of repression was valid and pragmatically very important. For instance, about a year and a half into a productive analysis, a patient (discussed in chaps. 4 and 5) began to dream about her inability to open tin cans without a key and about open coffee cans that were completely empty. Whatever had been openly available had been exhausted; the time had come to get at what had been sealed off. This turned out to refer to memories preceding the death of the analysand's father when she was just six years old. She said, "This is like Pandora's box; I don't want to face it—something monstrous is going to come out of it." No clearer statement could be made about the anxiety that sets repression in motion—nor about the resistance to further exploration it represents.

Several months of additional analytic work were required before the patient found a key to what had been repressed. This material began to appear in a dream she related at the start of a session, but half an hour later she suddenly realized that she could no longer remember the dream, her associations to it, or my responses to these. In fact, she could remember nothing about the analytic transactions of the entire past week. She thus repeated the childhood process whereby her forbidden wishes of the first six years of life had succumbed to amnesia. What then emerged was an erotic transference; about this, she said, "That I can now face my feelings is a great victory. . . I think it means that the analysis will be successful."

This clinical transaction was therapeutically crucial because it illuminated one aspect of the psychopathology—the tendency to shy away from dealing with conflictual issues by making a set of memories unavailable. In neuropsychological terms, this can only happen if input from (certain areas of) the left cerebral hemisphere is blocked (Basch 1983, Levin 1991, 2003). The most likely way this can be brought about is to make use of a lower level of organization— that of mode II, wherein the input of the right hemisphere is predominant. In the interval between her report of the dream and the onset of amnesia, the patient went through a period of altered consciousness (somnolence, as I then saw it) that probably marked the regression to an archaic mode of organization.[2]

Optimal adaptation is not possible as long as information that arouses anxiety tends not to be processed—that is, if it cannot be reconsidered in accord with novel life circumstances and additional knowledge. Because it is prima facie maladaptive, it is rather misleading to classify repression in adults as a defensive operation; yet insofar as a psychology centered on ego/id differentiation requires concepts of inhibiting structures that oppose the "drives," in that model of mind, repression *must* be defined as a defense. This contradiction constitutes a major objection to the validity of ego psychology.

Disavowal, Denial in Fantasy, and Isolation of Affect

Although disavowal (*Verleugnung*) was described by Freud (1927), its importance was not fully appreciated until Basch (1983) differentiated it from denial. The latter term refers to a cognitive error based on wishful thinking (A. Freud 1936); it always remains open to correction by confrontation with reality, in or out of treatment. Disavowal is a more complicated phenomenon. It does not involve any cognitive error—the subject continues to be cognizant of the facts, but their true emotional significance is disavowed. Because the facts are held to have no significance, the distress they should cause does not arise. For instance, a pain-filled true self may be disavowed so that the individual might avoid unpleasure by means of living as a false self. Such persons may seek assistance because they feel inauthentic, largely empty of genuine emotion. If confronted with the actualities of their inner lives, these patients will literally shrug them off.

If in analytic treatment such patients gain access to the dysphoric true self, they usually begin to disavow the import of the false self. Even Winnicott's (1954) choice of this term partakes of such disavowal, for it is not the adult capacities of the individual that are false—they are perfectly genuine components of the behavioral repertory. Modell (1992) has made the cogent proposal that the term *private self* is preferable to *true self*; by extension the *false self* should be called the *public self*. In any case, whenever portions of self-organization are kept apart—the unintegrated condition often called *splitting*—the significance of any of these may be disavowed in turn, depending on which nucleus of function happens to be acknowledged ("owned") at the moment.

From an ego psychological vantage point, disavowal (like repression) would have to be considered a mechanism of defense; from a therapeutic perspective, it is surely one of resistance. From an adaptive point of view, however (again like repression), it constitutes a disruption of intrapsychic communication. By averting appropriate affective responses to the actualities, it derails accurate assessment of the person's circumstances. Children resort to these ultimately counterproductive emergency measures because at the time they have no other way of avoiding potential traumatic states.

Disavowal should not be confused with *isolation of affect*, a different mechanism of defense described by Anna Freud (1936). This term refers to a condition of flattened emotionality that involves the individual's entire experience. In parallel with the neuropsychology of repression, isolation of affect may be brought about through exclusion of input from relevant portions of the right cerebral hemisphere. In the analytic situation, patients who suffer from this condition tend to intellectualize, that is, to talk about themselves in impersonal, quasi-theoretical terms. A variant of the syndrome is *alexithymia*, a lack of emotion caused by an inability to recognize one's own affective reactions (Krystal 1988)—that is, a failure to connect automatically generated affective reactions with the words that symbolize them. In either form, derailment of affectivity in the direction of overcontrol indicates maldevelopment at very early stages of maturation, involving the organization of the inhibitory structures of the ventromedial surface of the prefrontal cortex of the right hemisphere (Schore 1994).

Disavowal involves neither alexithymia nor inhibition of affectivity; the individual is generally able to experience emotions appropriately. It is the appropriateness of reacting to certain circumstances with emotion that is negated through disavowal. The distinctions among denial in fantasy, disavowal, and isolation of affect may be easier to grasp through clinical illustrations. Let us begin with a case of denial in fantasy.

Early in the second year of treatment, the analysand, for the first time in her existence began to experience real mourning for her father, who had died when she was six years old. In that context, she started to talk about having the power to have all her wishes granted through prayer.

> "I believe in God's power!"
>
> "You are kidding! You are really talking about your own magic."
>
> "Yesterday I prayed to my father to intercede for me with God. I used to pray to him when I wanted something too trivial to turn to God Himself. The teachings of the Church seemed to sanction this, but it started before I knew anything about Catholicism. The idea came to me that I could still talk to my Daddy. This way he is mine! I won't tell anybody, and they won't be able to take him from me. He won't forsake me any more—that is, he won't do it again. THIS SOUNDS WILD!"
>
> "Well—it's like the thinking of a six year old."
>
> "Yes, it has been submerged in me ever since . . . "
>
> "A private religion of your own."

As soon as the childhood fantasy of possessing a living father emerged in her associations, the analysand spontaneously repudiated it. At the same time, she failed to acknowledge that she had illusions of omnipotence—the actual significance of the magical thinking in childhood continued to be disavowed. Only about a year later did she stop dismissing all evidence of her grandiose illusions. She began to complain about the failure of her efforts to induce me to abandon the analytic role:

"You're not a real person! What's the use of getting angry—you won't change . . . "

"It won't change me, but it may change you."

"As a child, I used to play a game; I took it very seriously. I played it with grown-up men: I tried to knock them down. I felt very helpless and frustrated because I hit them as hard as I could, and they wouldn't budge."

A few days later, she had a frustrating dream in which her wish that the wife of someone should have died failed to come true. In another dream, she refused to ask for something she could have had for the asking. Her association was to the Magdalene, who did not dare to be open about touching Christ's garments: she could only do it when He was not looking. In other words, she knew that she vainly yearned for the absolute. She began to recall her childhood illusions about magical powers:

"When I was combing someone's hair, I thought that if I wanted it badly enough, I could turn straight hair into curly hair. The notion that I could change you was also a magical idea. When I don't see you, on weekends, the frustration builds up; I can't hold on to omnipotence any more, and I become really angry. Today I feel it's useless to try to change you—the reality here is *so* painful!"

"You shy away from the reality because you are afraid that your anger could magically destroy me, too."

"It was a coincidence! I wasn't responsible for father's death, even though I was angry!"

"Of course. The question is whether you knew that as a child."

"I don't remember, but I always felt I was the worst of children, just a terrible person."

She had to disavow that she felt guilty of murder.

Isolation of affect cannot be illustrated through an excerpt from this same analysis, for this patient had never lost touch with her affectivity. The best example I can offer is that of a middle-aged professional man who actually sought assistance because of deepening but vague dysphoria, apparently brought on by his decision, because of the risk of HIV infection, to stop using prostitutes to enact sadomasochistic scenarios. In the treatment, he was immediately relieved, for no discernible reason, and affective engagement did not take place. I sought to overcome this stasis by recommending an analytic schedule of four sessions a week, to which he gave his verbal agreement. Shortly thereafter, while on a brief vacation, he got so enraged (about having to accommodate his wife about a minor matter) that he threw a chair against the wall. He was very frightened by this loss of affective and behavioral control; he recalled that he had become a rageful child shortly after his mother gave birth to twins when he was four years old. He then decided that he should try to deal with his potential dysphoria through a psychopharmacological approach. Because he was vulnerable to dangerous breakdowns of his decades-long avoidance of genuine feelings (especially if he could not engage in secret rebellion), his choice may have been justified.

Projection and Projective Identification

Projection is a ubiquitous measure to avoid discomfort by attributing one's flaws to someone else. This is simply a cognitive mistake, albeit one motivated by self-interest. Its defensive function was particularly noted in paranoid conditions: Freud (1911b) postulated an etiological formula for these as "I don't hate you; you hate me." One does not have to lapse into psychosis, however, to make use of projection. It is quite common for analysands to fear that the analyst will make sexual advances to them when they are on the verge of experiencing an erotic transference. (I don't love you; you love me.)

Melanie Klein (1946, 1957) deserves credit for describing a process she called *projective identification* that has its origins extremely early in development and becomes manifest at certain junctures in analysis when matters referable to those phases of childhood are emerging. The term *projective identification* was an unfortunate choice (because the process differs from both projection and identification), but it has been so widely accepted that there is no prospect of altering the usage. It refers to a specific type of transference reaction in which a transaction from the era preceding full verbal competence is being repeated with a *reversal of roles*. The analysand enacts the role of the childhood caretaker, thereby inducing in the analyst the affective responses that characterized that childhood experience. This is not a prelinguistic manner of *communicating* with the analyst but a manifestation of repetition compulsion: self-cohesion requires endless reliving of the same drama. In analysis, usually it can only be repeated through reversal, for analysts are always careful not to reenact the potentially damaging behaviors of caretakers. (For an unfortunate exception to this generalization, see the first case vignette in chap. 4.)

Klein (1957) believed that in infancy the occurrence of projective identification *leads* to the confusion of self and object. This is only true insofar as continuing repetition of transactions in which such confusion was present naturally perpetuates that lack of clear differentiation. In this sense projective identification (in parallel with repression and disavowal) constitutes a breakdown in optimal information processing. In her conceptual work, Klein utterly disregarded evidence from cognitive science, which led to her arbitrary assumption that infants are able to conceive such entities as self and object. In actuality, such capacities gradually come on line in the second year of life; before such self-definition is achieved, infants retain memories of the affective consequences of experience while the roles of particular participants are not recorded. (For detailed discussion of such subsymbolic processing, see Bucci 1997.) In other words, projective identification is a mechanism that echoes the infant's inability to pin down the agent responsible for specific actions. Its persistence into adult life indicates that certain painful (even traumatic) transactions of infancy have remained split off as mere affectomotor schemata from those aspects of self-organization that eventually gained verbal encoding (Dorpat and Miller 1992). Its emergence in analysis should permit these matters to be processed symbolically, facilitating recontextualization (Modell 1990).

Occasionally, the resort to projective identification is of somewhat later origin. These instances occur when a child is so traumatized that a period of regression to archaic modes of organization follows, including loss of the capacity for symbolic processing. This was the case with the person I described in chapter 7 whose mother and sister brainwashed her; the traumatic events took place between the ages of two and four, after the departure of the patient's primary caretaker, a devoted nursemaid. Early in the analysis, the analysand verbally assaulted me on utterly preposterous grounds, so that I felt I was being driven crazy. Ultimately, I became aware that projective identification was operating; it was my ability to articulate how I experienced the transaction that allowed the patient to learn to process her past experience in a rational manner.

Withdrawal

The last maladaptive legacy of unfortunate "defensive" vicissitudes during early development is continuing resort to aversive behaviors—the constitutional propensity for withdrawal. If automatic resort to this tendency is built into the self-organization, the resultant personality structure is called schizoid. On an emergency basis, the ability to withdraw is available to all. Let me describe an instance in the course of the analysis already frequently cited.

> The threat the patient needed to avert was created by one of my minor therapeutic errors. We were discussing her inability to have both sexual and tender feelings for the same person:
>
> "I got very upset yesterday because [my lover] was being too tender."
> "It seems that you have the same attitude here with me."

Without seeming awareness, the patient literally moved as far from me as lying on the couch permitted. Such concrete bodily withdrawal is, of course, quite unusual, but this woman had avoided human intimacy for decades. She was thereby safeguarding people from the potentially murderous effects of her anger, inevitably provoked by disappointments in relationships. Consequently, it became impossible for her to learn what made her so unable to bear an ordinary human destiny.

Developmental Considerations

Regardless of the timing of their genesis, the various "mechanisms of defense," seen in analysis as resistances, remain permanently available as part of the individual's adaptive repertory, despite their overall disadvantages because they interfere with optimal information processing. As the cases I have offered seem to suggest, however, different mechanisms are characteristically employed when the various modes of organization that succeed each other in development are predominant. In mode IV, characterized by conflicts between infantile wishes and the standards learned from the caretakers, the most effective way to avoid anxiety is repression. In the realm of illusions that constitutes mode III, facts need not be forgotten; it is sufficient to disavow their emotional significance. In mode II, when symbolic processing is scarcely available, projective identification is likely to occur and will result in splitting off

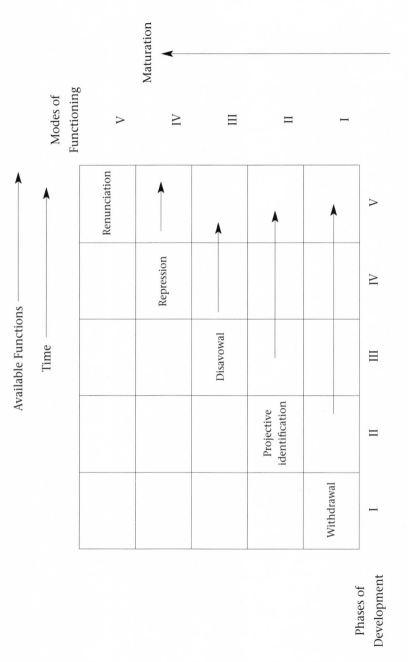

Figure 8.1. The development of defensive operations

crucial experiences from the realm of reason. In mode I, only constitutionally inborn biological operations are available; to avoid threats, that means withdrawal. This usually also involves changes in consciousness.

Summary

Whenever the steadily increasing intensity of affects threatens traumatization, this drastic outcome can be avoided through interruption of the usual intrapsychic communication of information. The various ways of effectuating these defensive measures are the specific mechanisms of defense discovered in psychoanalytic practice.

Differing neuropsychological explanations have been offered for the mechanisms of repression, disavowal, isolation of affect, projective identification, and withdrawal. Figure 8.1 portrays the correlation of the foregoing defensive measures with a hierarchical conception of the development of behavior regulation and of the central nervous system.

CHAPTER NINE

Affectivity

In *The Interpretation of Dreams* (Freud 1900), psychoanalytic theory became centered on the drives (*Trieben*). By postulating such inborn motivational forces, Freud believed he had anchored psychoanalysis to biology. With this step, psychoanalytic attention was diverted from the affects, albeit the problem of anxiety had previously attracted Freud's interest (1895b, 1895c). In Freud's ultimate efforts to revise his theories (1923, 1926), anxiety was again given a crucial role in neurosogenesis, but he had no satisfactory hypothesis to account for affectivity in general. Clinical work in psychoanalysis has never provided the kind of evidence on which such hypotheses could be based.

Adequate explanations of basic affectivity were finally proposed by Tomkins (1962–1963); they were first employed in psychoanalysis by Basch (1976). The work of Tomkins was summarized in one volume in 1995, and it has been extended by his followers, notably Ekman (1992; Ekman and Davidson 1994) and Izard (1991). According to these authors, affects are defined as the subjectively felt concomitants of various patterns of overall neural activity. Thus basic affectivity differs from the experience of pleasure or pain only with regard to the lack of known localization in the former, while the latter are known to emanate from specific centers. At any rate, affects are universal constitutional response patterns that become available in accord with a regular developmental plan determined by the progressive organization of the central nervous system. Basch (1976) suggested that emotions be differentiated from affects on the basis that an affect has to become symbolically encoded to qualify as emotion—the absence of such encoding constitutes alexithymia.

The Functions of Affectivity

According to the foregoing definition, affects are always conscious (in infancy, to whatever extent consciousness itself is operative). Consequently, they serve as signals that can guide the organism to take appropriate action to deal with the actualities that set off the affective response. In other words, affectivity becomes a cybernetic system of intrapsychic communication. In addition to their felt components, however, affective responses are accompanied by characteristic bodily changes; among these, facial expressions are of primary significance, for they can easily be read by others. Although not volitional, this is the infant's initial, automatic mode of communicating with caretakers (Muller 1996). Moreover, infants also have constitutionally determined automatic responses to perceptual input that reflects the caretaker's affectivity, such as the tone of a mother's voice or her facial expression indicating approval or disapproval (Schore 1994, Fonagy et al. 2002). These capacities permit caretakers to exercise some degree of control over the actions of children incapable of self-regulation. So-called affective attunement between infant and mother (Stern 1985) is this involvement of the caretaker in the cybernetic loop that guides the infant's behavior. The same semiotic system is available to all mammalian species. Panksepp (1998) suggests that the subjective component of affects forms the basis of consciousness.

In chapter 6, the establishment of a hierarchy of motivations in the course of the second year of life was postulated, without emphasizing that motivational priorities become structured only as a result of their usual affective consequences. Caretakers influence the organization of the brain and consequently of the self by intervening in a consistent manner to guide the infant's behavior. As Schore (1994) has described in detail, the caretaker's disapproval induces a shame response in the child. The neurochemicals produced as part of that response promote the development of inhibitory structure in the brain and lower the priority of the motivations that eventuated in shame, and so on. Later in development, the wishes that could lead to behavior that might shame the child (first through parental disapproval, then the child's own conscience) arouse anxiety, with ultimate neurosogenic consequences as postulated by Freud (1923, 1926).

The Control of Affects

The build-up of one of the affects to certain levels of intensity constitutes overstimulation from which the individual has no means of escape. In this regard, clinical observation has implicated shame, anger, and anxiety, in particular. By intensity of affect we mean not just a subjective sensation—more crucially, the accumulation in these circumstances of neurochemicals would eventually cause damage to nerve cells, particularly in the midbrain. Hence having the capacity to regress so as to interfere with normal consciousness— one of the consequences of traumatic disorganization—is, in emergencies, essential from an adaptive point of view. (To use an electrical analogy, it acts as would a circuit breaker.)

Let us recall the clinical example from chapter 7: the analysand who early in treatment kept "flipping out" did so because the benign environment in the analytic situation made her unbearably anxious. For example, the worst episode of "flipping out," lasting for several sessions, occurred when I indicated that I did not agree with her parents' assumptions that their own vocational choices were superior to every alternative. The patient simply could not integrate the prospect of a lack of opposition to her own preferences. Perhaps the best possible illustration of the point does not involve a treatment situation: during the 1944 landings in Normandy, a company of paratroopers was inadvertently dropped where it was completely surrounded by enemy forces. Thereupon, most of these seemingly doomed men reportedly went to sleep. Patients who become somnolent on the couch almost always feel threatened in similar fashion.

In adult life, individuals differ widely with regard to the intensity of affect they are able to tolerate. Frequent traumatization in the past, particularly in childhood, lowers the threshold of affect tolerance. These are the conditions found in persons subjected to excessive sexual stimulation as children before they have attained the capacity for orgasm. As Freud stated as early as 1894, such circumstances lead directly to mounting levels of anxiety. In adulthood, these individuals present the clinical picture of a posttraumatic stress disorder. In contrast, there are patients who are literally phobic about their emotions and avoid situations where these might be aroused. In its most extreme form, the avoidance of feeling can result in chronic boredom and a sense of emptiness.

Affective Disorders

The most severe disorders of affectivity are those wherein there is a defect in the ability to modulate emotional responses to the ordinary vicissitudes of life. Such an apraxia usually has a constitutionally determined component, but this is often reinforced by inappropriate affective training by the caretakers. One form of such maladaptive upbringing is a failure to teach the child to respond to an affect that has reached dangerous levels of intensity with behaviors that might diminish these. One analysand I worked with invariably responded to occasions of great joy by trying to redouble his pleasure. For example, one day when his work was to be recognized he arrived for his analytic session literally trembling with excitement, high on champagne. He complained of headache and photophobia, and he recounted that he had engaged in a fistfight with the taxi driver who had brought him. I had to show him how to calm down—as a first step, by predicting that if he did not "cool it" he would disgrace himself at the ceremony in his honor. As a small child, nobody had bothered to calm this person when he was careening out of emotional control. He still had to learn that enough is enough, and too much makes for trouble. Joyfulness is one thing, hypomania another.

In major affective disorders, similar defects in self-regulation will trigger neurochemical mechanisms that cannot be brought to a halt through simple interventions such as I have just illustrated. Depression or elation are merely the felt components of these profound biological disorders, which involve a host of vegetative functions with potentially life-threatening consequences— and not only by way of suicide. In many cases, the precipitating factor is the rupture of a preexisting symbiotic way of life; in such instances, the therapeutic provision of a new symbiosis will often reverse the neurochemical disorder. It may be more cogent to describe these situations the other way around: these are individuals who, in forming symbiotic attachments, have found an effective home remedy for their vulnerability to affective disorder.

To illustrate: a middle-aged intellectual sought help because his tyrannical spouse was about to leave him. In treatment, he insisted that I had to organize his life in the manner formerly managed by his wife. If I failed to comply to his satisfaction, he could still turn to her—or to one of a series of women he enlisted in the cause. He remained in equilibrium until my summer vacation, when his wife was also out of town. He did not disclose what kind of disorder ensued when he was left to his own devices, but the next time he felt abandoned in that way he fell into a profound agitated depression. He lost more than forty pounds in a few weeks. He refused the medication he was then given, and, within a few days of my return, his depression, with all of its physiological concomitants, disappeared. Although he had only contempt for my specific verbal interventions, the patient continued to hold on to the therapeutic symbiosis for a number of years, until his wife once more made herself available to him.

Complex Emotions

This clinical vignette points to the greatest weakness in our understanding of affectivity; the very terms used to designate particular affects are often imprecise. In this case, the clinical diagnosis of "depressive reaction" could be made on the basis of the consensually observed physiological symptoms, but the accompanying affective experience was never precisely determined. A variety of feeling states are vaguely called *depression.* In other words, depression is not a straightforward and simple subjective component of changes in the brain as are fear, anger, shame, joy, sadness, disgust, or surprise—the seven affects defined neurophysiologically by Tomkins and his group. Nor is this difficulty of defining emotional terms confined to depression. What exactly constitutes grief? How should we delimit bitterness? How about sympathy? Nostalgia? Love? Pride?

We seem to have a collective apraxia concerning definitions of complex emotional states. We can affirm, however, that such emotions always occur within an interpersonal context. It is therefore reasonable to postulate that they become available to children as developmental achievements that presuppose certain levels of cognitive maturation, particularly with regard to human relationships. One can only feel hatred on the basis of having made unfavorable judgments about someone who has the power to cause injury. Yet the subjective experience of hatred is absolutely unique—qualitatively as different from anger or contempt as colors differ from each other in visual perception. Such distinctions must necessarily reflect differentiated responses in the central nervous system. Neuroscientists have also differentiated the primary affective responses from the complex, secondary emotions that involve cortical participation (Damasio 1994).

A further complexity is that some emotions are almost always experienced as pleasurable and others as painful. Although such a classification breaks down in the instance of certain masochistic personalities, most people enjoy feeling love or sympathy and find it unpleasant to be envious or to experience guilt. This can only mean that emotions have the power, on their own, to recruit the centers of pleasure or pain to amplify the subjective experience they cause. It thus becomes understandable that in unusual circumstances a child may paradoxically find pleasure where others would feel pain and that the pleasure center might continue to be activated by analogous counterintuitive sentiments, for example, pride about failure.

Late in her analysis, I told one patient that she seemed to fear getting well because that would mean that analysis would be terminated. I added that actually all analyses end, whether they can be completed or not. She asked when such an end would occur.

"When it becomes clear that the analysis cannot be completed."

"Is that clear now?"

"No."

"Maybe if I work hard enough at it, I can make it clear! I am not going to do what other people expect!"

She had already told me that her great ambition was to be a successful failure: "That is the only thing I can be—a great Failure. That is my identity." There are families in which children are raised to compete for the honor of having suffered more than anyone else.

Affectivity and Therapeutics

By 1914, Freud concluded that it is insufficient for therapeutic purposes to make the unconscious conscious (1914a). He pointed out that, beyond interpretation, a process of "working through" (*Durcharbeiten*) is necessary to effect changes in adaptation. Subsequent psychoanalytic authors have almost never challenged this view, but until very recently nor has anyone attempted to substitute operational terms for Freud's metaphor. Previously, I suggested (Gedo 1995a) that the most significant aspects of working through are (1) the acquisition of new semiotic skills, (2) the expansion of "referential activity" (Bucci 1997), that is, correlation of primary and secondary process thought, and (3) the mastery of threatening unpleasure.

As far as I know, the literature on psychoanalytic technique has not addressed how such affective mastery can be promoted, but the oral tradition of analytic management has for generations included the prescription that, at the crucial junctures of affective crises in treatment, it is effective to point out to patients that the emotional intensities they were unable to tolerate as children are unlikely to be equally disorganizing in adult life. As Valenstein (1995) wryly noted, to call the process "suffering through" does not constitute a metaphor. It is also widely accepted that analysands are most willing to subject themselves to this kind of suffering in the overall context of a positive transference, for such reliving of the better aspects of the past gives analysands an illusion of safety—what Winnicott (1960) called a "holding environment."

Affective mastery most frequently involves a willingness gradually to permit experiencing increasing intensities of feeling; this is of particular importance in cases of chronic isolation of affect. There are, however, instances of inadequate affective control where the treatment most helps patients better to modulate some emotion. I have already given an example of a person who would deliberately try to escalate joy to dangerous heights; I have treated others who stoked their righteous anger until it culminated in ruinous confrontations. Self-destructive habits of these kinds are usually based on identifications with disturbed family members. The analyst may have to interrupt the rantings of enraged patients and convince them that venting anger will only heighten its intensity. Such a clinical dilemma demonstrates that affective mastery is often contingent on learning new ways to communicate—let us say, to explain what has caused one's injury instead of assaulting the offender. In other words, the curative step is to teach patients to use emotions as signals about their organismic needs and not to misuse them as weapons.

The clinical management of shame is even more difficult than that of anger. Kohut, in his work on narcissism (1971, 1977, 1984), taught analysts that it is counterproductive to shame patients into conformity with adult standards; people who suffer from infantile fixations are ashamed enough and are easily humiliated. With such people, the therapeutic task is empathically to focus on the *causes* of the infantilism and at all cost to avoid adding to their humiliation. Lack of therapeutic caution in this regard is one of the most frequent reasons for prematurely interrupted analyses.[1]

Working through the problem of an excessive propensity for shame generally requires clarification of patients' unrealistic expectations for themselves.

> An analysand who was never on time for her sessions reacted to one of the rare
> occasions when I nevertheless had to keep her waiting for a few minutes with an
> intense emotional outburst. She stormed out of my waiting room and returned
> five minutes after she had been told I would be available. In an unprecedentedly
> rude manner, she demanded an explanation for my lateness:
> "I am entitled to know why I was inconvenienced!"
> Several months later, the patient remembered her family's extreme poverty
> after the death of her father—deprivation that forced her mother to become a

washroom attendant at a public park. Whenever this history came up in a session, the following day she came even later than usual.

"Naturally I have come late when you bring that up! It means that I'm asserting that *I* am an important person, not a poor beggar. I have a right to come late— only the poor and unfortunate have to be early, to stand in line so there'll be food left for them in the soup kitchen. My sister is always late. Mother was never late. It is the privilege of aristocrats—nobody starts [in the absence of] an important person. Only the poor have to worry about hours."

After this, the patient no longer felt a need to be treated like a princess.

Summary

Affectivity has always been understood in biological terms. It is therefore not surprising that psychoanalysts have never been able to explain its mechanics on the basis of their clinical experience. Biologists have defined affects as constitutional response patterns that become available in a sequence determined by the maturation of the central nervous system.

Affectivity provides a cybernetic system of intrapsychic communication. In infancy, while executive control resides in the mother's mind, the cybernetic loop must be completed through the caretaker's ability to read the baby's affective signals and by affective attunement within the dyad. One of the caretaker's vital tasks is to teach the child appropriate measures that will regulate affective intensities. Control of this kind is lacking in major affective disorders. We are still unable to provide adequate explanations for the operation of complex emotions that occur in interpersonal contexts.

One of the curative measures in psychoanalytic treatment is the attunement of affective mastery through increasing degrees of affect tolerance.

CHAPTER TEN

Dreams and Dreaming

Freud considered *The Interpretation of Dreams* (1900) his best work—an opinion subsequently buttressed by the fact that its method of interpreting dreams has received almost no criticism. In the early years of psychoanalysis, deciphering dreams was considered to be "the royal road to the unconscious." This judgment was also justified, provided it is understood that dreams are a road to the elucidation of what has been repressed or disavowed subsequent to acquiring symbolic representation and to matters experienced in early life that never gained such symbolic encoding. In a different sense, dreams reported in psychoanalysis are (and have always been) conscious phenomena.

As already mentioned in chapter 1, Freud's enduring contribution in *The Interpretation of Dreams* was detailed description of the semiosis in dreaming, a language he called the "primary process" (Freud 1900, 588–609). Later, Freud (1911a) was to state that this is the language of the unconscious—an uncharacteristic error whereby he confounded the text of the manifest dream with the clues about "unconscious" mental contents latent within it. In addition, he mistakenly regarded the primary process as a primitive functional state (to which one putatively regresses in sleep); he postulated that in the course of maturation it is superseded by the "secondary process" of rational thought. Within psychoanalysis, Rapaport (1967) and Noy (1969) were first to articulate that primary and secondary processes have entirely separate lines of development. As cognitive scientists have shown (Bucci 1993), what psychoanalysis calls primary process is simply the language of the right cerebral hemisphere.

The Grammar of Dreams

Freud explicated the language of the dream in chapter 6 of *The Interpretation of Dreams* (1900, see esp. 509–87) by showing how the manifest content may be translated into the discursive language of the secondary process. He compared the dream to a pictographic script that may be deciphered image by image. (The same is true of Chinese ideograms.) Freud stressed that each image may simultaneously represent several ideas, an outcome he called "condensation." He assumed that defensive operations actively continue during dreaming, largely by means of a process of "displacement," whereby emphasis is shifted from crucial to less important elements in the imagery. Freud accounted for the occurrence of verbal material in dreams by assuming that these auditory percepts are also mere concrete signs, in exact analogy to their visual counterparts.

As contemporary cognitive psychologists see these phenomena, they constitute the usual thought processes of the right cerebral hemisphere. These are encoded not in verbal symbols but in a subsymbolic code (Bucci 1993, 1997). Such processing takes place by way of parallel channels for the various perceptual modalities. Hence the analysand's verbal account of a dream inevitably translates it into a code alien to it (Spence 1982)—this in large measure accounts for what Freud (1900) called "secondary revision," the transformation of a sequence of discrete images into a more or less coherent narrative.

In this view, dreams constitute efforts to process the meanings of current experience on a nonverbal level (Palombo 1978, Bucci 1997). They occur in those phases of sleep when rapid eye movements (REM) are present and the left cerebral hemisphere loses its dominant role. In such circumstances, affectivity emerges from under "the pale cast of thought" (as Shakespeare put it); that is why dreams are the best means of apprehending the crux of psychopathology. Archaic experiences, often never encoded in verbal form, can best be recalled in the form of dreams (Bollas 1987). Bollas has called information stored in this manner "the unthought known." As Dorpat has pointed out (in Dorpat and Miller 1992), it is no longer tenable to accept Freud's assumption that primary processes are cut off from reality.

The Function of Dreaming

Freud's (1900) understanding of dreaming was entirely biological. He assumed that, through creating "hallucinatory" wish fulfillment, dreaming carries out the vital function of preserving sleep. He was correct to postulate that sleep is a vital need, but he did not know that it is guaranteed by neural activity at the midbrain level rather than by illusory ideation. Dreaming must have profound evolutionary advantages, for it is the common property of all mammalians. Dreams and hallucinations are neural events; they are not caused by desires (Dorpat and Miller 1992).[1]

Sleep is a vital need because it permits regaining functional baselines at the neurochemical level. In this context, the biological function of dreaming is to promote that process by the achievement of affective equilibrium, through attempted recontextualization of troublesome experiences (see Modell 1990) by way of mobilizing the relevant affectomotor schemata. (These components of the self-organization are the procedural memories that constitute the sole record of the preverbal era.)

Dream Interpretation

Freud proposed a pragmatic method that is still in use for translating the meaning of dreams into consensual language. It slightly departs from a strict technique of free association because it requires voluntary focus on the dream, either as a whole or as a sequence of discrete elements, or both. (From the viewpoint of good clinical management, it is therefore not always indicated to pursue the interpretation of any and all dreams reported by patients, for such tactics may turn into a game of hide-and-seek that serves the resistance to change.)

Patients vary enormously in their ability to come up with associations to the dream (or its components) that will permit comprehension in rational terms. One measure of analytic progress is improvement in this regard, for it betokens better intrapsychic communication—"referential activity," as Bucci (1993) calls the ability to correlate primary and secondary processes. Analysts may be tempted to substitute their own associations for those patients may be unable to supply, but this is a highly risky procedure, for the significance of every individual's pictographs is almost wholly private.

In a productive analysis, the patient may learn to interweave dream interpretation and a focus on the transference so that both become easily understood with little intervention on the part of the analyst. Let me offer an example from the end of the third year of the analysis from which I have taken most of my illustrations.

Just before Christmas, the patient became preoccupied by W. B. Yeats' poem, "The Lake Isle of Innisfree." She said it expressed nostalgia for one's childhood home. She then reported a dream:

"I'm doing some secret work someplace, for my friend who is in analysis. I call my sister on the phone, and I won't tell her where I am. Afterwards, she calls back and asks, 'Is that you, April?' I say to myself, 'My God, how did she know I was here?'. . . The secret place is the analysis—I have only given your name to my sister and my boyfriend."

She then veered off the dream; in the next session she barely remembered it and only for a moment. She was quite late for the following appointment, and she became afraid that I would dismiss her from treatment as punishment for this offense. She related this fear to her mother's disapproval of lateness—mother was always early and waiting for her children.

"It's amazing how you have reproduced these circumstances with me: you come late enough so that I'm almost always waiting for you."

"When Daddy died, mother had a job as a washroom attendant at the park. I was desperate to hold on to her, and I could go to the park any time to be with her . . . That's what the analysis feels like; I had my mother all to myself there. I wish I could come here whenever I felt like it."

She began to cry.

"I had her to myself because the others were ashamed to see her at the washroom. It was such a lowly job! My sister was too fine a lady to appear at a washroom. I was so young, I didn't care what mother was doing—I wanted her! We had a special intimacy then that the others didn't share."

"The way you wanted to keep your sister away from here in the dream?"

In the next session, the patient expressed strongly hostile feelings about an attractive woman whom she saw leaving my office. And so on. The crucial association to the dream was not given just verbally but by way of the dramatic enactment of being afraid of punishment for her lateness.

I trust it is clear that, from a therapeutic perspective, elucidating this dream had almost no importance (although making the connection between the dream and the subsequent analytic material gave *me* some satisfaction)—what was significant was recognition of her continuing longing in waking life for an ever-available maternal person for whom she did not have to face any rival. She did not need my input to recognize these feelings, so interpreting the dream only served to confirm *for me* that she had gained insight into the manner in which she was repeating the past in the analysis.

This analysand, an eager student of poetry, had ample referential skill and seldom failed to discern the meaning of her dreams. Poetry, more than any other human discipline, depends on the simultaneous manipulation of primary and secondary processes.[2] For other patients, the acquisition of such skills can be slow and frustrating. I illustrate these difficulties with a brief excerpt from a case history I published many years ago (Gedo 1984, chap. 4).

Shortly after he started analysis, a young psychotherapist dreamed that a large turtle was participating in a football game. The animal was stealthily carrying the ball inside its carapace; its opponents failed to realize this, so the turtle was creeping unimpeded toward the goal-line. The patient realized that the turtle referred to him, for he had been a star ballcarrier as a high-school football player. It took many months for him to connect the concealment of the ball to his deliberate withholding of various associations in the analysis, and years passed before he realized that he viewed treatment as a competition with me. Of course, this man's handicap extended beyond making sense of the pictographs in dreams—he was equally incapable of grasping the meaning of narratives in movies. In Bucci's terms, he was almost incapable of referential activity.

Dreams and the World of Early Childhood

Freud (1900, 189–220) correctly observed that dreams are related to the subject's early life—as he put it (with less justification), they represent the fulfillment of infantile wishes. The two examples above show what he had in mind: the woman's dream contained a wish for exclusive and unconditional access to her mother (albeit this wish was *not* gratified in the dream); the "turtle" wished, by fair means or foul, to defeat his male rivals. This correlation to the childhood past is not merely a consequence of immersion in an analytic process—it is also found in dreams reported in extratherapeutic contexts. I can only illustrate this observation through one of my own dreams.[3] It occurred the night before I flew to New York to deliver a named lecture for a prestigious psychoanalytic audience.

In the dream, I was the New York Yankee pitcher Ron Guidry, warming up to start the World Series at Yankee Stadium. An interviewer asked whether it was true that I had the best fastball in the business. I replied, "I don't know. We'll see." This answer gratified me intensely. Of the numerous associations that I had to the dream, the most relevant were that my father had been a star athlete, but *Guidry* (in his time) had arguably been the best in the business. How about myself? (*Gedo*). I had been raised by a deluded mother to believe that I was destined to be best. The intense pleasure at the denouement was produced by the fact that I no longer shared my mother's delusion.

I believe the dream represented mastery of the tendency to yield to temptations to become grandiose. Thus it dealt with the current status of the lifelong issue of self-assessment on the basis of irrational criteria accepted at the dawn of self-awareness. (In terms of Freud's contention about the fulfillment of childhood wishes in dreams, it was my wish for autonomy with regard to ideals and ambitions that was gratified.)

All three of my examples buttress Bucci's (1997) contention that dreams process the meaning of human experience, especially (I would add) in terms of its affective consequences. New experience evokes affects in accord with its relation to the established self-organization—such as the turtle's rigid defensive armor or my freshly acquired indifference to the expectations of others. The core of the self-organization is laid down in the form of affectomotor schemata (procedural memories) prior to the acquisition of symbolic capacities. (These developments have already been described in chap. 6.) To consider fully the meaning of current experience always necessitates placing it into the context of its bearing on this core of the self. I assume that this is the reason for the finding that dreams always involve the evocation of the preverbal era.

Dreams and the Sense of Reality

Freud (1900, 426–59) insisted that rational thinking within dreams is carried over wholesale from secondary process thoughts that preceded dream formation. In view of current explanations of dreams as products of the right hemisphere, Freud's two-stage hypothesis no longer makes sense. It is therefore no paradox that dreams may involve complex intellectual operations, such as my patient's awareness (in the dream about her sister's intrusion into the analytic space) that it was indeed known where she could be reached while she was working with me. Reports about scientific conclusions that were reached in the course of dreaming have become legendary—witness Kekulé's conceptualization of the benzene ring by way of a dream in which a snake was swallowing its own tail. What such incidents should actually tell us is that creative thinking necessarily has to make use of the primary process and subsequent referential activity.

Another way to look upon this issue is to keep in mind that even in REM sleep the prefrontal cortex / left hemisphere is never really unavailable—it is merely dormant because its input is generally not needed. If rational judgments should become desirable, they can be made. (Best in the business? "I don't know; we'll see.") The best evidence for this contention is that dreamers almost always know that they are dreaming. Should they lose sight of this reality, they tend to comment on this strange experience in their report of that dream, "It was so vivid that I thought it was real!" (Conversely, if damage to the cortex, as in Alzheimer's disease, impairs the capacity for rationality, patients become unable to distinguish between dream and waking experience.)

Dreams that seem "real" come close to the experience of waking hallucinations—although the sense of reality is not universally absent when a person is hallucinating, either. One may have visions (or hear voices) and be quite aware that they are unreal. The sense of reality is invariably lost in those dreams classified as nightmares, in which mounting anxiety spills over into panic. Of course, in such conditions the fear is very real indeed. The same is true of the occurrence of orgasm in the course of dreaming. In both instances, organismic reactions mediated through the midbrain have been mobilized. Yet it should be kept in mind that it is also possible to dream that one is in panic or is having an orgasm, only to awaken with the realization that the experience was *not* real.

The Dream in Clinical Practice

Because the mode of action of psychoanalysis is no longer seen as a matter of making the unconscious conscious, the former concentration on dream interpretation in clinical practice has, naturally but all too gradually, dissipated. Analysands probably report dreams with undiminished frequency, but there is less pressure to pursue the royal road to the unconscious. Analysts therefore tend to allow free association to proceed where it will, instead of insisting on an associative focus on the undeciphered dream. It has become apparent to most clinicians that the report of lengthy or numerous dreams and the effort to "understand" them is generally in the service of resistance. Moreover, the interpretation of dreams, even if valid in its own right, often leads to surprising unintended consequences (Gedo 1981, chap. 3). It is easy to lose one's way on the royal road.

One of the most valuable aspects of translating dream-hieroglyphs into consensual (verbal) language is that the procedure itself, cumbersome as it is, can teach the analysand the most reliable method of referential activity. At the very least, it should convince even skeptics about the efficacy of the associative process in that regard. The lesson is applicable not only to dreams but to all unexamined aspects of mental life. It generally becomes apparent over the course of an analysis that the patient's dreams tend to deal with the most pressing issues of current existence, especially with regard to their affective consequences. (In their verbal accounts of dreams, analysands often neglect to mention that they experience a variety of emotions while dreaming, but they are generally able to specify what they felt if the analyst asks for that information.)

It is therefore most effective therapeutically to correlate the significance of the dream(s) with the patient's immediate life situation. The childhood precedents for the current emotional responses to specific circumstances may fruitfully be discussed at some point, but it is counterproductive to make dream interpretations that overlook the present because of some antiquarian preoccupation with the past. A brief illustration may best show how a dream can illuminate an analysand's actual status.

After a considerable amount of work, I could not conceal my impatience with this patient's adherence to the status quo in a severely dysfunctional marriage. He responded with a dream in which he was following the best friend of his adolescence in doing something completely backwards. Reluctantly, he associated that his friend was a clever delinquent and a gambler. Thereafter, he paid no attention to the dream and talked in a disconnected manner about a number of matters. I commented that his approach to the dream reminded me of his description of his friend's attitude to life: it was cavalier and lacking in attention to detail. He agreed, with some enthusiasm, and began to talk about his unwillingness to use what he had learned in the analysis to lessen the friction with his wife. He then associated to a science fiction movie in which a man with magical powers was engaged in rescuing a regal woman. He was only interested in adaptive change if he could bring it about through magic.

Summary

Dreams are manifestations of the predominance of right hemisphere functioning during sleep. They normally occur in all mammalians as one aspect of the continued neural processing of those waking-life events that have impinged on the individual. Hence Freud was mistaken in thinking that dreams are cut off from reality. By mobilizing relevant affectomotor schemata, dreaming promotes the process of regaining functional baselines (at the neurochemical level) through the attempted achievement of affective equilibrium.

Freud devised an effective method for translating the meaning of dreams into consensual language. There is great individual variation in the ability to learn to carry out this task of interpretation. Dreams provide an entry into the emotional world of early childhood, which is largely encoded in nonverbal schemata. Nevertheless, the dreamer almost always retains a sense of reality: "This is only a dream." Dream interpretation retains its clinical usefulness, provided it is employed to illuminate the patient's current life situation.

CHAPTER ELEVEN

The Biopsychology of Early Experience

In adult life, we have no verbally encoded memories of infancy; as one consequence, human psychology is generally apprehended in terms of thoughts formulated in symbols. Everyone knows, of course, that such a conception is invalid—human beings only acquired spoken language relatively recently in the history of the species. Moreover, infants communicate pretty well during the preverbal era. Lacan (1977) has given this fact the utmost emphasis; he believed that the acquisition of spoken language actually alienates us from our true humanity. In my view, such alienation is a pathological development of relatively infrequent occurrence—most people do not live their lives in accord with a false self. Nonetheless, in certain instances, Lacan's claim is valid; he was also correct in pointing out that analysands may engage in "empty speech"— language devoid of significance that covers over all matters of actual importance that lack verbal encoding.

Disavowal of the archaic, nonverbal self is tempting—especially for psychoanalysts, whose therapeutic method relies almost exclusively on verbal communication! Perhaps the prevalence of mentalist theories in psychoanalysis reflects such a reluctance to tackle the legacies of our preverbal past and our continuing nonverbal present. Until relatively recently, all the competing developmental hypotheses within psychoanalysis attributed to infants the capacity for conceptual thought that is acquired only through the use of symbols. The core of our humanity is, however, lacking in such encoding.

That is not to say that the preverbal infant has no cognitive or semiotic skills. Because human development is epigenetic, these archaic modes of operation persist throughout the life-span, albeit they may be difficult to observe in everyday life. The psychoanalytic situation, however, provides optimal circumstances in which to note the occurrence of resort to these archaic capacities. In chapter 6, I gave several dramatic examples of the emergence of such behaviors, such as actual babbling or the experience of impending disorgani-

zation in terms of concrete bodily sensations. Many more illustrations are offered in my book *The Languages of Psychoanalysis* (Gedo 1996).

Recognition of these archaic forms of cognition and semiosis provide the
analytic observer with tools that illuminate the biopsychology of early experience. To make optimal use of these observations, we should keep abreast of
the advances in cognitive psychology and semiotics. (Recent summaries of
these were presented to the psychoanalytic community by Bucci [1997] and
Muller [1996], respectively.) These disciplines belong within natural science,
and their conclusions can serve to anchor psychoanalysis in that realm; at the
same time, the clinical utility of these conclusions is more immediately apparent than that of the neurophysiology underlying them. (Unfortunately,
many clinicians cannot see the relevance of brain functions for psychoanalytic
work. See, for instance, Smith 1997.)

From a clinical perspective, it is of primary importance not to confuse the
occurrence of preverbal semiosis and/or presymbolic cognition with symptoms
that possess symbolic significance (that is, with conversion reactions [Breuer
and Freud 1895, chap. 3]). It is true that, in certain instances, seeming regression to such archaic functional states is motivated by some transferential attitude—let us say by a wish to puzzle or to provoke the analyst—but in most cases
it is simply an automatic resort to the adaptive repertory of infancy. As such,
it is most likely to occur when the analysis has succeeded in mobilizing those
archaic issues that are of greatest significance in the patient's maladaptation.

Let us return to the analysand I described in chapter 7, the patient who lost
her primary caretaker at age two and was subsequently abused in a number of
different ways, sadistic and sexual, by several people. The most damaging aspect of this persecution was an older sister's attempt at "brainwashing," which
actually undermined the patient's confidence in her own capacity to test reality. At the same time, she learned that words can be misused to manipulate
and torture people—that, by itself, verbal communication cannot be relied on.
Hence she paid special attention to the language of gestures, one much more
difficult to falsify.

In the analysis, this woman had the tendency to communicate the most
fundamental matters wordlessly. I had great difficulty in deciphering these
messages, but I did eventually grasp the meaning of the ones that she repeated
most frequently. The most dramatic enactment of this kind was the patient's
propensity to run out into the hallway in the middle of her sessions. (I practiced in an apartment in a large residential building; during my office hours,

the hallways were deserted.) Before the scheduled hour was up, she invariably returned, without explanation. Eventually, we realized that she was conveying through this dramatic scenario what her infantile experience had been when she could not understand the comings and goings of her beloved nursemaid (who disappeared every weekend). Her psychopathology in this regard consisted of her inability to translate the significance of her activities into consensual language. In other words, she could not understand her own behavior. (This example also demonstrates the tremendous adaptive advantages entailed in acquiring verbal competence—few interlocutors would have failed promptly to understand her point had she been able to put it into words.)

Protolinguistic Phenomena in Psychoanalysis

Nonverbal semiosis is not an infrequent phenomenon in clinical psychoanalysis, and it is almost always of real significance for the individual's pathology—at the very least, because the inability to encode certain matters verbally has profound adaptive disadvantages. As Muller (1996) has noted, the preverbal child engages in a variety of "protolinguistic" communicative behaviors—as, of course, do animals; gestures and bodily postures constitute one of these "zoosemiotic" systems.

Levin (1991) has reviewed the progressive evolution of human semiosis. In his schema, the first component of that repertory is the language of affects, partly conveyed through vocalization and facial expressions. The language of gestures and postures is added next. Isolated words that, like images, possess consensual meaning begin to amplify communication later in infancy, but "anthroposemiosis" is not fully established until the child is able to use syntactically organized language. In adults, the various components of the repertory form an integrated assembly that can selectively employ any of these capacities.

Clearly, analysands generally use all components of the semiotic repertory in the process of free association, most prominently the paraverbal aspects of speech. The protolinguistic phenomena I next discuss differ from such optimal verbal communication, although this difference may be hard to detect because the analysand may continue to articulate seemingly meaningful words. The significant meanings of such communications may only be discerned by focusing on the music of the analysand's speech. The occurrence of such a protolinguistic episode presents a therapeutic challenge because the analysand simultaneously loses the ability to judge whether these messages are comprehensible; the crisis may be compounded because the patient may also be unable to comprehend the analyst's communications.

In the most dramatic instance of this kind I encountered in practice, such regressive loss of verbal competence constituted the reliving of profound regressive episodes (in response to a series of traumatic disruptions of relationships to caretakers) between the ages of two and four. As long as this person remained unable to put his feelings of rage and despair into words, this alexithymia condemned him to endless reenactments of the regressive pattern. The "music" of the enactment could take two forms: it could be provocative or neutral. The former denoted the vengefulness of an abused child; the second mode turned out to mean that the analysand expected me omnisciently to read his mind. At any rate, I had to make the distinction on the basis of my response in the countertransference.

Regressive loss of the ability to communicate meaning may in some instances be covered over by blathering—what Lacan termed empty speech. One person who realized that such behavior severely jeopardized the chances of therapeutic success complained that his words invariably falsified his authentic inner experience. This person was able to discuss someone else's emotional life in the most sophisticated of vocabularies but was unable to correlate the same words with his own affects.

Other patients may lapse into silence, not because they are withholding associations but because they have no verbally encoded thoughts. Often these silences are punctuated by involuntary motor acts such as loss of sphincter control, vomiting, diarrhea, orgasm, or convulsions. Muller (1996) called attention to the equivalence of these phenomena to the vocalizations of infants; consequently, they have been referred to as "sign-babbling." (In this context, *sign* denotes that these acts do not have symbolic meaning but do point at some concrete significance, as does, for instance, a flashing light.) When analysands recover from these states of wordlessness, they describe having felt bewildered and "empty"—stunned. These experiences repeat homologous childhood conditions.

The Language of the Body

In the course of psychoanalysis, several distinct kinds of somatic symptomatology may emerge. In conversion reactions, some body part has assumed an unconscious symbolic meaning that leads to an experience wherein a scenario is enacted using that part in the assigned symbolic sense—let us say hysterical blindness as a punishment for prohibited voyeurism: "If thine eye offend thee, pluck it out!" Stress reactions constitute a second category of bodily symptomatology; migraine, epilepsy, neurodermatitis, and mucous colitis are common examples of that kind. The stress generally produces chronic, unrelieved affect; if some organ system is constitutionally vulnerable, it will in these circumstances malfunction.

Here I wish to focus on bodily symptoms that do not belong to either of the categories just described. These are somatizations without symbolic referents that constitute communications by means of the concrete signals for which gestures and/or facial expressions can be used. Tics are the simplest form of such bodily signaling. The tiqueur remains unaware of the message encoded in these actions; from the perspective of his consciousness, they are passively endured. The intentionality of the tic has never had symbolic representation.

Hypochondriasis is another instance of a bodily signal (often a mere memory of some somatic event)—one that is utterly misread by the sender, who concludes that it is a symptom of tissue pathology. The signal is conveyed by means of the sensory apparatus so that only the sender is able to detect it. In adult life, of course, the message that something is seriously amiss is then communicated to others verbally. Nonetheless, the sensation is an essentially autistic experience and an illustration of the concreteness of infantile mentation. In the treatment, it may be possible to help patients read the meanings of their sensations correctly. A (hypochondriacal) substernal pain, misread as a heart attack, may signify that an impending event threatens some vital interest of the individual. In other words, even an autistic phenomenon may be dealt with as a potential interpersonal communication by translating it into consensual language. Such a procedure amounts to the correction of an apraxia by way of direct instruction.

Altered States of Consciousness

Other phenomena referable to the preverbal era of childhood that may manifest themselves in the psychoanalytic situation are altered states of consciousness. These can only emerge in states of profound regression that temporarily set aside the dominant self-organization so that a hitherto split-off segment of the personality comes into focus. In my clinical experience, events of that kind are relatively rare, for the adult form of consciousness comes on line rather early in infancy (Hadley [1996] conjectures that this occurs with the functional development of the amygdala at around three months of age)—consequently, thereafter altered states of consciousness constitute regression from a previous developmental achievement. In other words, in adults, even regressions to the earliest modes of psychic functioning may preserve normal consciousness; the alterations occasionally observed in the clinical situation reproduce early childhood conditions of malfunction—generally as part of (repeated) traumatic experiences.

In chapter 7, I discussed the need to suspend normal consciousness in the midst of disorganizing experiences. I there described two patients who reexperienced such states in my presence. The only other analysand I worked with who had similar episodes characterized them, on regaining the ability to describe her subjectivity, as "being lost in a fog." Her report described not an absence of consciousness but a state of bewilderment; contact with the outside world had been interrupted. The necessities of effective treatment usually preclude systematic inquiry into the phenomenology of these dire events—one must, instead, focus on their precipitants and how to avoid repeating them. I suspect that this phenomenology would, if collected, prove to be rather varied, depending on which of the numerous functions of the mind/brain that add up to normal consciousness have been impaired. Being "lost in a fog" and "flipping out" (another analysand's characterization of her experience) are almost certainly different states of organization from the conditions that must prevail in disorders such as "multiple personality" or enduring amnesias.[1] And all of these differ from the states of apathy and emptiness that French colleagues have labeled *"l'espace blanc"* (blank space). Dreams, of course, represent still another distinct form of consciousness (see chapter 10).[2]

The Compulsion to Repeat

The tendency to repeat maladaptive behaviors referable to early childhood was noted by Freud (1920); recently, it has been attributed to the absolute need to maintain the core of the self-organization established in the preverbal era (Gedo 1979, 1988). As Freud correctly noted, this biological need has priority over pleasure-seeking—it is "beyond the pleasure principle." Because the compulsion to repeat even maladaptive aspects of early behavior patterns will cause pain and loss, Freud postulated that human biology is characterized by "primary masochism." This formulation illegitimately overlooks that early patterns embedded in the self-organization are also continually repeated if they produce pleasure and profit.

I should like to provide a clinical illustration of compulsive repetition that produced pain and pleasure, in alternation.[3] This patient started life with severe infantile eczema that produced unbearable itching; this led to scratching, rage, and finally exhaustion—a pattern carefully recorded in a baby book by an appropriately concerned mother. In the analysis, the entire sequence was exactly repeated early in the second year of our work when, following a case of shingles, he experienced a severe exacerbation of dermatitis. Although he was very uncomfortable, the patient made no move to get expert dermatological assistance. Instead, the symptom seemed to "join in the conversation" (Ferenczi 1912) within the analysis: he expected me to relieve his symptoms, and because I failed to intervene, he engaged in furious scratching. His itching was stimulated by various kinds of pleasurable excitement, in the analytic setting and elsewhere. Ultimately I was able to point out that he lent himself to going through a cycle of excitement, overstimulation, rage, helplessness, autoaggressive activity, and exhaustion. He then consulted a dermatologist who was able to bring the dermatitis under control. The patient thereupon felt bewildered—estranged from his real self.

Needless to say, when the condition of his skin did not lend itself to such exact repetition of past experience, this highly intelligent person was able to find ways to reproduce the same cycle of sensations by other means—they were the leitmotifs of his existence. For example, as an adolescent he was ever ready to fall in love, but, because any positive response sent him into raptures, he invariably disrupted the relationship so that frustration, rage, and despair ensued. A few years later, he learned to reproduce the mortification of his flesh as well by taking up smoking, which exacerbated his bronchial asthma.

I believe we all live our lives in this manner—we are merely ignorant of our leitmotif because it has not been recorded in a reliable baby book.

Summary

Psychoanalytic treatment often permits observation of the biological bedrock of behavior regulation that is entirely independent from verbally encoded thinking and constitutes the core of individuality. Hence analysts must be prepared to recognize the meanings of archaic (nonverbal) forms of cognition and semiosis, such as nonverbal enactments, the paraverbal aspects of speech, blathering, involuntary motor acts, stress reactions, bodily signals (often misperceived as somatic pathology), and altered states of consciousness. Even more crucial is apprehension of those compulsive repetitions that manifest the need to maintain the basic organization of the self-system.

CHAPTER TWELVE

Disorders of Thought

Magical Thinking and Delusions

The most common cognitive disorder encountered in psychoanalysis is magical thinking. So frequent is it that for many years it was widely regarded as a normal phase in the development of thought; its appearance in adulthood was therefore conceptualized as regression to an early functional mode. Alternatively, it could be seen as the persistence of primitiveness in cognition in a split-off segment of the personality—a view that appeared to explain why many analysands used magical thinking only about selected matters.

Take, for instance, a patient about to terminate an unusually felicitous analysis who, only some weeks before the scheduled end, revealed that she engaged in a daily ritual (an afternoon nap and before-dinner drink) that she looked upon as essential for her well-being.[1] As she reconsidered this so-called habit, this very sober person realized that this was a piece of personal magic, and the prospect of giving it up filled her with anxiety. Ultimately she decided to opt for rationality and the relinquishment of this illusion of invulnerability. As she did so, we discovered that she had learned these magical tricks from her admired mother; obviously, she could not exactly follow the formula until she herself became a woman of leisure. Note, however, that the pathogenic idea, preserved for decades through disavowal, was formulated in terms of rather sophisticated abstractions such as health, privilege, and well-being. In other words, this nucleus of magical thinking was formed at a relatively advanced stage of cognition. (Stern [1985] rightly pointed out that magical thinking must *of necessity* use symbolic capacities.)

This clinical vignette supports the conclusion of Rapaport that magical thinking "is a 'theoretical' system and as such is organized in terms of a synthetic function alien to the primary processes . . . demonstrating that [this kind of] thought and [such] practices involve secondary processes" (1967, 842–43). In other words, magical thinking has to be learned through interactions with the caretakers in the developmental phase that follows the acquisition of symbolic capacities. These interactions often involve explicit instruction—for instance, indoctrination in the magical efficacy of prayer; in other instances, adherence to magic comes about through identification with the ways of the parent.

Some observers have objected to these conclusions because young children, when left to their own devices, will sometimes engage in risky behaviors that may be misinterpreted as reflections of grandiosity. Such interpretations are illegitimately adultomorphic: these children are initially simply ignorant about the nature of things as well as of their own limits. It is up to the caretakers to respond to the child's mistakes about these matters in a way that will give the youngster accurate feedback concerning the realities. Failure to receive correct information will mislead the child into unrealistic expectations about what is possible.

Although there is no psychoanalytic consensus on this score—for instance, Kohut (1971, 1977, 1984) and his followers still look upon grandiosity as an expectable phase in cognitive development—in my judgment such magical ideation is not primarily biologically determined but is the consequence of miseducation. Grandiosity is a pathological phenomenon, albeit it is regrettably common. It is, however, true that such personal magic is usually hidden behind a false self of later origin that presents a more rational public facade.

It is also possible to rationalize grandiosity by misusing socially sanctioned religious beliefs as a cover for what amounts to a private religion. In chapter 8, I give an example of such a contingency: the analysand had convinced herself that her belief that she had the power to have all her wishes granted through prayer conformed with her church's teachings. In that instance, magical thinking was relinquished when the patient was confronted by the voice of reason. Such an outcome is expectable when the resort to magic is encountered without additional disorders of thought, particularly delusional complications.

That way of stating the matter is actually circular, for unrealistic beliefs are classified as delusions precisely when they prove to be unalterable by confrontation with reality. Such an unfavorable outcome occasionally may be caused by poor therapeutic technique; nonetheless, in most cases it is a function of something about the patient that trumps rational arguments. Let me give an example. A highly accomplished academic came to me for a second attempt to be analyzed that turned out to be no more successful than the first. We persevered long enough to discover that the patient had an unshakable conviction (ordinarily disavowed) that he alone possessed the truth that it is impossible to attain reliable knowledge. For analysis, this constituted checkmate. *Nothing* I could say counted for anything; I was discredited in his eyes by my evident faith in science.

Here was a megalomaniac delusion ("I alone understand") based on another delusion ("nothing is valid"). Like a binary star, the two were interconnected in a manner that precluded changing either one. The megalomania had been learned at his mother's knee; her own grandiosity had been overt and ubiquitous. Yet she was not a nihilist, and my patient arrived at his bizarre epistemic convictions on his own. (Certainly, very little he heard from his mother was valid!) The certitude that transforms a mistaken idea into a delusion betokens a miscarriage of the neural functions that subserve reality testing. This is clearly so in the major psychoses caused by biological disequilibria, and it is also true in delusions formed by nonpsychotic individuals. These are the people Hamlet calls mad "only north-northwest."

Or only from midnight until one A.M. Such temporary lapses into delusion, observable in certain analyses (hence sometimes designated as *transference psychoses*), demonstrate that delusion formation is a regressive phenomenon—a return to the neurophysiological arrangements of the preverbal era. In those cases where treatment weathers such a regressive crisis, the episode constitutes a therapeutically necessary reliving of an experience that in childhood could not be symbolically encoded.

For instance, a highly intelligent analysand reacted to an inaccurate intervention on my part by hallucinating a fecal odor; he was delusionally certain that this emanated from me. (I had stunk up the place!) He became very frightened at the thought that I was out of control and for a couple of days was unable to come for his appointments. He finally phoned me and realized that he must have misinterpreted events when he registered my calm tone of voice. Upon resumption of our work, we discovered that in this transference enactment he had reversed roles. As an infant, he had suffered from chronic, foul-smelling diarrhea; the unbearable disgust he experienced toward me was an echo of his mother's feelings about her disgusting child. (This is an illustration of the transactions Kleinians call projective identification.) The only unusual feature of this repetition of the past was that it encompassed the denial of reality on the part of his mother, who could never admit her ambivalence about her defective son. Although he was merely repeating such a denial of reality, at the same time he reverted to concretized thinking (a stinking performance qua odor) and could not for the moment distinguish his private thoughts from external events. In an adult, an infantile inability to test reality constitutes a delusion.

Obsessional Thought

Obsessionality is a complex disorder; its cardinal features are doubt and ambivalence, doing and undoing, isolation of affect, and intellectualization. Magical thinking is also frequently present but does not constitute an invariable component of the syndrome. Reversing one's actions is, of course, the all-but-inevitable consequence of pervasive doubting, and compensatory intellectualization naturally follows the lack of availability of one's affectivity as a guide for behavior. Doubt, moreover, is also likely to occur if one cannot determine how one feels about the available choices. Thus isolation of affect (discussed in chap. 8) may well be the central feature of obsessions—a necessary but insufficient condition of their genesis, for it does not always lead to this syndrome.

Lack of complete access to one's subjectivity dictates using external criteria for one's choices, for instance, the opinions of prestigious authorities, public fashion, and so on. The difficulty of such a Rube Goldberg apparatus is that there are so many competing authorities with differing opinions—obsessionals need external guidance to make a choice. They fall into an infinite regress of ambivalence about the very process of making a decision, and the matters these unfortunates tend overtly to obsess about are usually quite trivial. (Do I need to buy black shoes or brown? Shall I go to the shoe store on Friday or Saturday?)

The isolation of affect in these cases need not be absolute: they can certainly experience humiliation, envy, and contempt. Obsessionals are barred access to certain affectively charged aspects of the presymbolic self-organization that constitute vital components of their being. In all probability, this access did not get barred through regression but was never established in the first place—in circumstances Freud (1915c) labeled "primary repression." Although the obsessional personality remains unable to apprehend these matters, the primitive affectivity in question continues in active operation and may be registered by reliable observers. A clinical example may illuminate these conditions.[2]

An intellectually gifted young man was referred to me for a third attempt at analysis; the first two had been discontinued in acts of undoing. He was largely paralyzed by trivial obsessions, and his existence was organized to avoid humiliation by impersonating a man of high sophistication. He was getting desperate about leading such a sterile and fraudulent life. Despite his bewilderment, patient analytic work eventually brought to light the genesis of his illness.

The patient was the oldest of four children born within a span of five years to parents who for the most part delegated the care of this brood to domestics. By the time he was three years old, this child was so jealous of the latest nurse-maid's care of the newest baby that he locked her out of the house. His physical attacks on his siblings were severely punished. Later in childhood, he realized that his mother's first love was her dog; when the opportunity presented itself, he did away with the animal. Yet he never realized that he was waging a relentless war against his mother—that his true self was suffused with a need for vengeance. Consciously, he thought she was pitiful, helpless, at worst ridiculous.

What lacked symbolic encoding was not so much his hostility (for instance, he was well aware of hostile competition with his brother); rather, he had no conception of his pervasive sadism. He mistreated women but could not understand why they complained. Nor did he grasp that he preferred failure as part of a scorched-earth policy to frustrate his highly ambitious mother. Focusing his thoughts on trivialities helped him to avoid the sole important issue of his existence, his Thirty Years' War against her. In this sense, not only was his crucial affectivity isolated—so was his rational judgment. He was unable to distinguish what was truly important, and this apraxia rendered him incapable of planning his behavior. In other words, the output of his left prefrontal cortex was unconnected to those aspects of his personality that were structured in the preverbal era. In the clinical situation, his obsessions increased in frequency and took on a vengeful flavor whenever he felt abandoned by me—but he had difficulty understanding my conclusion that he was avenging himself by submitting me to a torrent of meaningless verbiage. (Feces?)

Other cases have been reported in which, despite comparable derailments in development, the dominant aspects of the personality managed to experience a more or less expectable oedipal crisis. The anxieties stirred up by this situation then caused regression to the functional modes of the split-off obsessional core. Essentially, this was the formulation Freud (1909b) offered to explain the pathogenesis in his celebrated case of the Rat Man. That certain obsessional cases can be looked upon as neuroses (that is, manifestations of intrapsychic conflict) while others are better understood as personality disorders stemming from the preverbal era shows that obsessionality is a heterogeneous diagnostic category.

Consequently, it should cause no surprise that the syndrome may also result from primary abnormalities (probably of more than one kind) in brain function. Such conditions are not likely to be encountered by psychoanalysts. For example, damage to the basal ganglia may interfere with screening out irrelevant information, leading to a kind of tangentiality in verbal communication that mimics the doubt and undoing of the obsessional. A different organic etiology is at work in individuals subject to the major psychoses who sometimes attempt to prevent complete disorganization by obsessional preoccupation with some familiar notion.

The last possibility is probably also at work in young children subjected to severe stress shortly after having formed their core self-organization. The dispositions I have described in the man who was perpetually at war with his mother probably jelled in that manner. This amounted to the adaptive use of the barely acquired capacity for verbal reflection in a highly unusual manner that abandons rationality. If this adaptation forestalls disorganization, the child may be able to dispense with the assistance of the unreliable caretakers who have failed to provide a satisfactory milieu.[3]

Focal Disorders in Thinking

In addition to the cognitive pathologies already discussed, there exists a wide variety of thinking disorders focused on specific functions and therefore less pervasive in their effects than magical thinking, obsessionality, or delusions. The most familiar example of such a focal apraxia is the defect we call the lack of a sense of humor. This designation does not refer to an inability to experience the complex affective state of mirth—individuals who cannot appreciate humor are often moved to laughter by the fulfillment of some sadistic wish. (The Germans have a word for this, *Schadenfreude*—malicious joy at another's misfortune.)

At any rate, having no "sense of humor" is a cognitive rather than an affective deficit. I suspect it may come about in a number of different ways; the one I am most familiar with is literal-mindedness. Humor can only be grasped by decoding the speaker's rhetorical devices (tropes). Those unable to do so may simply be deficient in verbal intelligence (for any number of constitutional reasons affecting the brain), but the deficiency can also come about as a result of lack of appropriate stimulation. Among patients of high intelligence, I have observed similar literalness in those who learned to distrust verbal communication because in childhood it was misused to manipulate them. (Incidentally, these are the analysands with whom it is too risky to employ humor in treatment. They may experience it as ridicule or look upon it as levity inappropriate in dealing with their tragic situation.) In still other cases, a pall of depression makes it impossible to regard anything as comical.

A much more unusual syndrome involving a cognitive deficit is the inability to grasp the implications of various kinds of human transactions. In chapter 10, I mention one analysand who could not grasp the narrative line of the movies he attended—he was no better at apprehending the meaning of the behaviors of his own family members. Yet this man had an excellent record as a student; the apraxia did not extend to the comprehension of written materials. It was basic human transactions that baffled him because they were unconnected to the familiar words that describe them in texts. (The defect is analogous to the inability to recognize one's affects in alexithymia.)

I believe this cognitive deficit was, in this instance, caused by a lack of exposure to these elementary aspects of what it means to be a human-among-humans during the critical period when such matters are usually learned as affectomotor schemata. This person was so grossly understimulated that the resultant childhood apathy eventually led to a lengthy hospitalization. At that time, the pediatricians recommended as the sole therapeutic measure that his mother pay him greater attention. Very likely it was only the child's excellent native endowment that saved him from even more extensive developmental failure.

I provide only one further illustration of a cognitive disorder, that of an inability to trust one's sense of reality. In the most egregious instance of this problem I encountered in my practice, the analysand had been subjected, for a number of years following her acquisition of consensual language, to a regime of brainwashing. (I discuss the traumatic consequences of these experiences in chap. 7). When she complained to her mother that her older sister had abused her physically, the response she got was not mere disbelief but an active effort to persuade her that she had misinterpreted the relevant events. Faced by a united front of mother and sister, the youngster learned that she had best refrain from reaching conclusions on the basis of her subjectivity. In this manner, her system of internal feedback, necessary to evaluate her circumstances, was put out of commission.[4]

Summary

Disorders of thought may be caused by biological abnormalities, but in some instances they are acquired as a result of erroneous instruction by caretakers. A very common consequence of such miseducation is the persistence (often disavowed) of magical thinking. Because this involves the use of symbolic capacities, it is organized in terms of the secondary process; it is *not* an archaic phase of normal development. By contrast, delusions usually constitute a regressive return to the neurophysiological organizational mode of the preverbal era, although in some instances they may merely constitute an identification with a delusional parent. Obsessional disorders may be caused by a wide spectrum of etiological factors, from dysfunctions of the basal ganglia to adaptation to early childhood stress by a combination of isolation of affect and reliance on toying with verbally encoded ideas that have become structured at a neural level. Certain focal disorders of cognition are apraxias caused by a lack of appropriate stimulation or the avoidance of certain stimuli that proved to be potentially dangerous.

CHAPTER THIRTEEN

Object Relations

Among the concepts of psychoanalytic theory, perhaps none has been as variously defined as that of *object relations*. Introduced by Freud (1905b, chap. 3) in the sense of a person toward whom sexual desire is directed, the term *object* came to denote anyone with whom the relationship assumed a libidinal aspect. Because Freud (1905b, chap, 2) classified pregenital sensuality as a behavioral manifestation of libido, the concept of sexual objects was, in his system, applicable even to the nursling's attachment to its mother. In these terms, an object relationship was seen as a transaction in the realm of actual interpersonal activity. The concept continues to be employed in this sense, most significantly to refer to the relationship between patient and analyst.

It is no longer assumed a priori that the therapeutic relationship is primarily erotic in nature. Perhaps the clearest example of this change of conceptualization is provided by Kohut (1971, 1977, 1984), who discerned that many analysands formed a vital and tenacious bond to the analyst that had little or no sexual connotation. Instead, these patients require that the therapist perform for them certain psychological services, such as providing positive feedback about their personal merits. Because such services presuppose that the analyst has suspended the exercise of his or her personal volition, Kohut postulated that these patients experience the therapist-as-object as part of their own psychic self; hence he chose to call this type of relationship one to a *self-object*. I give an example of such a state of affairs in chapter 6, where I present the dream of an analysand who was contemplating termination. In that dream, she equated the prospective loss of the analyst with the amputation of a limb.[1]

Relational Theories versus Attachment-as-biology

Despite the continuing use of the concept of object relations in the interpersonal sense, recent psychoanalytic theories more frequently have focused on the intrapsychic correlates of these overt phenomena. These are the structured psychic dispositions manifested as transferences in the process of analytic treatment (as I demonstrate in chap. 4). Influential theorists—most no-tably Winnicott—have focused on these unconscious structures as the cardinal vectors that determine adaptation and maladaptation. Theories of that kind have been called "relational" (Greenberg and Mitchell 1983). They are based on the assumption that early object relations (in the interpersonal arena) are "internalized" so as to form a variety of "internal objects" in continuing transaction with representations of the self. Mitchell (1988) went so far as to claim that the mind is "composed" of such relational configurations.

It is hard to believe that Mitchell meant this claim to be taken literally (in what way is one's store of knowledge, from arithmetic through foreign languages to psychoanalytic theory, a relational configuration?), but it is worth considering what caused him to make such an extravagant statement. Because psychoanalysis takes place in a dyadic setting calculated to evoke the analy-sand's repertory of relational configurations, the content of patients' associa-tions tends to focus on such matters, more and more so as an analysis makes progress. Mitchell overlooked that his analysands lived most of their lives in solitude.

It is rather difficult to learn how patients function on their own through psychoanalytic methods, which continuously provide a holding environment. Psychoanalysis is inherently more intrusive than is a good-enough mother, who generally provides her infant with sufficient experience of being "alone in the presence of the mother" (Sander 1980). Analysts seldom leave their pa-tients the "open space" required for optimal learning (Sander 1983). Gardner (1983) has, however, proposed to counter the passivity forced upon analysands by the traditional methods of psychoanalysis by encouraging patients actively to process their own associations.

Even early childhood experience is largely solitary, as Winnicott (1951) rec-ognized when he described "transitional phenomena." Relational theories tend to emphasize the lasting influence of memories of dyadic transactions on sub-sequent behavior. As I stated in chapter 4, such conclusions are the result of illegitimately equating the emergence of various transferences in the course of analysis with the analysand's pathological inability to learn better ways to adapt. Beyond this erroneous assumption, the relational viewpoint almost uni-versally neglects to consider how human attachments are formed in the first place (but see Greenberg 1991). Consequently, object relations theorists are ever tempted to adopt the mentalist viewpoint—as Summers (1994) put it, to be content with "pure psychology."

Yet the absolute need for enduring relatedness between mother and infant in all mammalian species shows that attachment is a biological issue. As Harlow (1962) long ago demonstrated, monkeys should have simian caretakers. The greatest contribution of psychoanalysis in the realm of public health was the work of Spitz (1946), who showed the devastating (even life-threatening) effects on human infants in old-fashioned orphanage settings of the lack of any stable relationship. This achievement was extended by Bowlby's (1969) observational studies on the attachment needs of infants.

As I have already mentioned in chapter 6, Lichtenberg (1989) was right to conclude that attachment is one of the independent motivational systems already active at birth. The neonate's attachment behaviors reciprocally activate a corresponding maternal attachment. Like lactation, this propensity is potentiated hormonally. If the mother-infant dyad constitutes an "average expectable environment" (Hartmann 1939), the ensuing object relationship yields experiences forming regular patterns impregnated with affect that get laid down as procedural memories of affectomotor schemata. These are the generalized representations of actions Stern (1985) calls *RIGS*. At this early stage of development the infant cannot have any concept of "mother," so the idea that it is an "object" that is internalized is mistaken. The infant acquires "know-how," not a representation of the caretaker. As Lichtenberg (1983) pointed out, mental representations of others can only be formed when, around the middle of the second year of life, the capacity for semantic memory begins to be acquired.

If attachment to the primary caretaker leads to steadily painful consequences, the infant's only recourse may be to withdraw from the noxious relationship. The schizoid state that results has been most thoroughly studied by Guntrip (1968). Such a true self may be covered over by a facade of relatedness that is only an "as if" simulacrum. What is truly damaging in such cases is not the individual's disinclination to form genuine new attachments but the failure to have acquired the requisite know-how about the basic requirements of human existence.

Take the case of the painfully obsessional man briefly described in chapter 12. He seemed to manage adequately as long as he was organized by external requirements (such as a class schedule), and he was very good, indeed, as a guerilla fighter. Left to his own devices, however, he became helpless. For instance, on a solo vacation in Paris, he took refuge in a bookstore where he spent the day obsessing about the reading he might do in the future. Early in the analysis, when he had "free" time, he lay around his apartment in an apathetic daze. In other words, he needed someone else to set priorities among his various wishes and the long-term program to fulfill his declared goals.

An apraxia this profound compels the affected person to seek out assistance from whoever may be willing to lend it. What (from the viewpoint of an external observer) may look like the resultant symbiosis does not amount to an attachment to an object (or, if you will, to a "selfobject")—to the schizoid individual it makes no difference at all who provides the assistance. These helpers are used as prostheses and are as casually discarded as a soiled bandage. (If analytic treatment with such patients is to have any chance of success, the first order of business must be to make certain, by being continuously helpful to the apraxic person, that the analyst will not be discarded.)[2]

In contrast to the inability of the schizoid personality to form genuine attachments, individuals whose difficulties had their origin in traumas or deprivations that followed the consolidation of their self-organization will, in properly managed analyses, reexperience their early attachments as transferences. I may best be able to convey the flavor of the emergence of such intrapsychic dispositions through the example of an analysand who was abruptly separated from her primary caretaker (because of inescapable external events) when she was about two years old.[3]

This woman rather quickly established a transference that repeated the positive attachment of her infancy. Early in the analysis, whenever our work was interrupted, she *felt* helpless but soon recovered by taking refuge in haughty aloofness. Later, she experienced the analytic relationship as indispensable and felt anxious about any possibility of separation from me; moreover, she felt humiliated by any lack of availability on my part. Late in the treatment, her positive feelings reached a peak that exceeded my ability to empathize. On the day preceding a long Christmas weekend, she failed to arrive but phoned about fifteen minutes after the scheduled starting time. She announced, in some distress, that she had been held up by a traffic bottleneck; she estimated that she could not get to my office for more than five minutes of her session. I assumed that she was seeking confirmation for a decision to avoid about an hour of driving, back and forth, for the sake of a pro forma appearance for her session. I told her that I understood how much she would regret having missed the last visit before Christmas. She never entirely forgave me for this failure to grasp that no amount of effort and trouble was too great to make even the briefest contact with me possible. Still, she eventually accepted my failure as the inevitable limitation of a mere man who could not be expected to know anything about mothering.

One-person versus Two-person Psychologies

The relational paradigm is currently favored by a plurality of clinicians, probably because most patients presently in treatment suffer from character disorders that somewhat impair their personal autonomy so that they become dependent on the analyst. As a result of such a bias in sampling, psychoanalysts see relatively few persons who "suffer the slings and arrows of outrageous fortune" in the mind alone. The phenomenology observed in the analytic situation has led many practitioners to stress the ubiquity of dyadic transactions, such as the events I have just described. This preference is, in a way, understandable, for the transferences they have the opportunity to observe are seldom mere matters of love and hate—they manifest various imperative needs for human assistance. In the case just discussed, the analysand needed continued reconfirmation of her worth—that is, that she did not deserve to be discarded. As Anna Freud (1965) put this, reliance on the object is a way station on the developmental line from helplessness to autonomy (see also Gedo and Goldberg 1973, chap. 5).

Sigmund Freud disregarded the need to study object relations because of a sampling bias opposite the one currently common: he selected patients for analysis only if their development had successfully transcended the need for external assistance. The psychoanalytic theory he propounded (Freud 1923), portrayed in the tripartite model of ego/id/superego, focused exclusively on the intrapsychic world—in contemporary terms, it was a one-person psychology.

Both Freud's theories and the object relations theory developed to replace them are grossly reductionistic. Some authors, such as Kernberg (1976) and Loewald (1989), have tried to make complementary use of both theoretical systems, but these syncretic efforts have only led to confusion. As I have repeatedly stated (most recently in Gedo 1999, chap. 18), a theory centered on a concept of self-organization should be able to encompass all of the data previously dealt with by those competing reductionistic theories, without running into the insoluble problem of correlating their entirely distinct concepts. (For another discussion of this issue, see Gedo 1981, chap. 8.)

At the same time, theories focused on the self-organization have an exclusively intrapsychic focus. Among other matters, they deal with the characteristic manner in which the individual processes relationships taking place on the stage of actuality as reflections of affectomotor patterns acquired in early life. Before the consolidation of self-organization, another person must continuously be involved in the regulation of the infant's behavior. As Freedman (1997) pointed out, however, the infant's attachment to the primary caretaker does not yield memories of a relationship but only those of a sequence of subjective experiences. (As the French say, one must live one's life within one's own skin.)

Nonhuman Objects

Winnicott (1951) was the first to note that young children may actively perpetuate certain infantile experiences wherein they have full control over what happens; he called such experiences *transitional.* He chose the term because the materials the child used in this manner had been named *transitional objects,* for Winnicott regarded these as substitutes for the (uncontrollable) primary object. Children are strongly attached to these transitional objects—more precisely, they need to repeat the familiar experience they can at will actively recreate by their means. In the course of expectable development, the transitional object is outgrown and discarded. Because infants have no concept of "mother," Winnicott was plainly mistaken in regarding the transitional object (say a blanket or a soft toy) as a mother substitute. The matter is better understood as an active repetition of subjective experience that can only be passively received from the mother as she chooses. Hence the implication that a nonhuman thing may provide an object relationship for the infant is misleading. The transitional phenomenon creates that "open space" within which the infant practices for autonomous competence in solitude. Perhaps the transitional activity that persists longest is the masturbation of the oedipal child, albeit this is often accompanied by fantasies that do concern a human sexual object.

In circumstances that impose more than ordinary helplessness on a young child, phenomena analogous to transitional experiences using inanimate things may occur beyond the preverbal era. In such cases, the child attributes magical properties to some inanimate object which then becomes essential for the maintenance of psychological integrity. Greenacre (1969) proposed calling these special things "infantile fetishes," in analogy to the fetishes worshipped in certain tribal religions. The power of a fetish depends on attributing omnipotence to it; in fantasy, the worshipper gains power (overcomes helplessness) by virtue of a special bond to the magical thing.[4]

The use of such apotropaic magic is not to be confused with fetishism as a sexual perversion (a topic discussed in chap. 14 with other permutations of sexuality).

Reconstructions of the Past in Psychoanalysis

It cannot be too strongly emphasized that the emergence of a specific transference in the course of treatment can only be used to reconstruct the analysand's *psychological* world at a particular period of childhood; it does *not* constitute evidence about the actualities of the person's past history (Spence 1982). When, after some years of analytic work, a very intelligent woman finally reexperienced an archaic mother transference, we realized that, very soon after she had acquired language, the patient was strongly convinced that her mother was dangerously hostile to her. It took a great deal of further effort to establish that this childhood conviction had been entirely mistaken. This childish error resulted from misinterpretation of the mother's dangerous *incompetence* as deliberate policy: the daughter could not conceive until she reached the age of eleven that her parent was grossly damaged. (It was quite a feat on her part even to discern, in the third year of life, that she was not being treated right!)

This same analysis demonstrated that a person's characteristic modes of relating to objects in adult life may develop relatively late. The analysand was strongly invested in being helpful to people in need, especially children. This character trait reflected an identification with a supportive female relative who died when the patient was not yet five years old. It first manifested itself in her devotion to a brother who was born shortly after that loss. The patient as an adult also manifested a second relational pattern: a profoundly masochistic self-abasement and unrealistic idealization of the object. This characteristic was consolidated even later than her altruism; it developed after she started school, when her father deserted the family, and she was left with only her impaired mother to rely on. She managed not to fall into despair by creating parallel illusions about mother's merits and her own deficits. Both character traits were self-created to meet a variety of emotional needs—they were not products of automatic internalizations of an object, as relational theories would imply.[5]

Summary

Object relations, understood in an interpersonal sense (for instance, as the analyst-patient relationship), form an important component of all psycho-analytic theories. In contrast, the currently popular "object relations theories" illegitimately elevate the intrapsychic representations of past object relations to the role of the exclusive agents of mental activity—a conception termed a *two-person psychology.* Attachment is one of the inborn motivations of the human organism, but infants register only affectomotor schemata as a result of transactions with caretakers, not representations of objects. The intrapsychic world is therefore inevitably best conceptualized by a "one-person psychology," that of self-organization.

On those terms, so-called transitional objects are not substitutes for an absent mother; the infant engages in transitional activities in order to actively recreate experiences previously passively received by way of the actions of the caretakers. In a clinical context, it is crucial not to assume that the analytic transference is a repetition of actual events in the past: it is, rather, the recreation of past conditions in the intrapsychic world.

CHAPTER FOURTEEN

Permutations of Sexuality

All schools of psychoanalysis have agreed that sexuality is a biological phenomenon that plays a highly significant role in human psychology. In itself, this truism has allowed a great variety of competing hypotheses to flourish— from the pansexualism implicit prior to 1920 in some versions of drive theory to mentalist conceptions that equate the role of sexuality with that of any other subjectively experienced bodily capacity (such as, for instance, locomotion).

Probably no other topic relevant for psychoanalysis is as fraught with cultural bias as is sexuality. At the close of the Victorian era, when psychoanalysis was born, the antisexual attitudes prevalent in bourgeois circles caused more intrapsychic conflict about childhood sexual manifestations in Freud's clientele than we are likely to encounter nowadays; homosexuality and the perversions, until recently classified as pathological, are widely accepted today as statistically expectable variants. Despite this "sexual revolution," psychoanalysis must discern the precise roles of nature and nurture in producing such sexual permutations.

In his major statement on the subject, Freud confessed (1905c, chap. 3) that science was ignorant about the sources of sexual excitation. Although it is now understood that it depends partly on the production of sex hormones and (at least in animals) on the presence of pheromones, we still do not fully understand why certain levels of these are necessary and/or sufficient in some cases but not in others. Pornographic images emit no pheromones, but they stimulate many individuals; that specific imagery will be sexually exciting for some but not for others demonstrates that something beyond hormonal levels must be involved in the process—very likely whatever the image means to the individual. Stoller (1975) has cogently argued that the reasons for the evocation of sexual feeling by particular stimuli is a major gap in the psychoanalytic understanding of human psychology. The difficulty is compounded by the fact that one cannot easily ascertain whether a subject is stimulated by an external percept or by a concurrent internal fantasy. Having sex with a person of one gender does not exclude the possibility that in fantasy the other gender is creating the excitement. (This capacity to use fantasy to improve upon the actualities probably accounts for the increased frequency of homosexual contacts wherever the opposite sex is unavailable.)

At the same time, it is certainly true that the vast majority of people respond with sexual excitement to more or less identical stimuli. (For instance, certain behaviors are widely regarded as sexually provocative. This can only mean that exposure to such behaviors will excite numerous people.) This finding strongly suggests that a sexual response to certain percepts is constitutionally determined. (Representations of the nude female until quite recently never included the depiction of pubic hair, thereby reducing their power to excite the viewer.) Yet particular thoughts and emotions may override such automatic responses; witness the imperviousness of adequate health care professionals to the very same percepts they would find stimulating in private life.

Perhaps I have said enough to show the enormous complexity of this entire topic. In order to decrease its difficulty, Freud (1905c) proposed to separate it into issues involving the choice of a sexual object and those dealing with the "aim" of sexual behavior. In the first category, Freud mentioned hetero- or homosexual object choice, as well as pedophilia and zoophilia. In the second, he listed various nongenital goals that lead to orgasm (all of which may be pursued with persons of either sex).[1]

Homosexuality

The homosexual community was certainly justified to oppose the classification of same-sex object choice as an illness, for it is a most heterogeneous phenomenon. Some individuals are exclusively homosexual, others are bisexual. Certain people are homosexual at particular periods of life or in specific circumstances, others from quite early in childhood remain so steadily throughout the life span. It therefore is extremely unlikely that (as some extremists claim on inadequate grounds) homosexuality is simply caused by some genetic variation. The clinical experience of psychoanalysts has thus far been too limited to permit valid generalizations to be made on that basis: obviously, only those "homosexuals" seek analytic assistance who know themselves to be psychologically ill (in a broader sense than that of choice of sexual object). It is not clear how far it may be legitimate to extrapolate from findings in this subgroup to those who have not been observed in the psychoanalytic situation.[2]

Despite this caveat, the gender of the preferred sexual object of adult life almost certainly is determined by the psychological outcome of the childhood developmental crisis called "the Oedipus complex." It was an oversimplification to summarize this (as was often done in the past) as a predominant identification with one parent or the other—an identification that supposedly included that parent's sexual orientation. Children "identify" with their caretakers by learning discrete adaptive skills from them; these bits of desirable behavior do not (and cannot) include what to be sexually aroused about. Rather, the oedipal crisis impels the child to erotize to a greater degree the relationship to one or the other parent—that is, to crystallize *wishes* for bodily intimacy with a man or a woman. (Usually there are wishes for both, but one tends to predominate.) The vectors that swing the balance in either direction are manifold; they are frequently matters that were structured as psychological dispositions at earlier stages of development. To cite only the simplest of examples, if an individual's gender identity differs from that person's actual sex (a matter usually determined in the preverbal era), the individual will be predisposed toward a same-sex erotic choice.

That example, of course, occurs relatively rarely. I believe a more common pattern is the one I encountered in the three analyses of homosexuals I conducted (or, in one instance, supervised).[3] All were males who emerged from the oedipal crisis with profound fear of and hatred for women, attitudes determined by transference responses to potential sexual partners. The care of one boy was entrusted to an intrusive and controlling grandmother, allegedly because his mother was fully absorbed by the needs of her alcoholic husband. When the child was five, his mother had another baby—a girl whom she nursed with loving care. This circumstance overwhelmed the boy with such hatred that he literally made a pact with the Devil (a living presence for this pious family). Understandably, he also wished he had been born female. He longed in vain for succor from his father, by whom he was consistently rebuffed. It was in this situation that he began to feel sexually excited by males he could idealize.

In adult life, this person could not remain faithful to a very decent and caring (male) lover—he was chronically fearful about being enmeshed in a stifling relationship such as the one with his grandmother. He engaged in repeated episodes of wild promiscuity (with multiple sexual partners) that restored his ever-deficient self-esteem because he was the star of the gay orgies he frequented. He established this pattern in early adolescence; it amounted to a home remedy for his dysphoria. In these sexual encounters, he treated his partners as animate tools—in other words, he was engaging in a fetishistic perversion.[4]

There are doubtless other patterns of nurture that lead to the same outcome, following the oedipal situation. Moreover, one must consider the influence of constitutional dispositions on the choice of sexual object—in a multifactorial system, other things being equal, every factor may be decisive. To illustrate: the second homosexual analysand I treated did not have to cope with the unmanageable family situation of the first man. His mother did try to force him into a symbiosis and to exploit the talented child for her own narcissistic gain, but his father was not impaired in any way. The father did reject the child when the latter turned to him, and he made it clear that what put him off was the boy's effeminacy. This may well have been genetically determined.

Perversions

Almost a hundred years ago, Freud (1905c, chap. 1) tried to define perversions as patterns of sexual behavior that are habitually (rather than occasionally) preferred to sexual intercourse. That definition is not fully satisfactory, for it does not cover sadistic acts in the context of coitus, the use of fetishes to make intercourse possible, and similar behaviors that use genital congress to achieve primarily nongenital aims. The best way at present to restate Freud's proposition is to define as perversion any action that recruits the sexual system for ends that are *not* erotic. Stoller (1975) came close to that definition when he claimed that perversion is the erotic form of hatred. That statement is clearly valid for sexual acts of a sadistic nature, but it is not self-evident that the nonerotic motivation of other perversions necessarily involves hatred, although it may do so in individual cases.

Thus, the old hypothesis that masochism is merely the turning of hatred against oneself greatly oversimplifies the etiology of the syndrome. In the instance of masochistic perversion I have most fully analyzed, what superficially looked like sexual humiliation turned out to have the meaning of a narcissistic triumph—analogous to the sense of irresistible attractiveness achieved by the homosexual analysand who was numero uno in the gay bagnios. In the case of my patient, the masochistic perversion fulfilled a grandiose fantasy. I would not dare to estimate how frequently these dynamics underlie the syndrome, but I am confident that masochism may have a variety of other meanings, including self-hatred. A dynamic of grandiosity may also produce various other syndromes—let us say exhibitionism or voyeurism.

The correlation between perverse behavior and narcissistic pathology was noted by Kohut (1971, 1977). His writings on the topic focus exclusively on the analysand's subjectivity, so he described this connection as a pragmatic device the affected person has found to deal with the severe dysphoria caused by narcissistic injury—a condition Kohut described as the felt threat of impending "fragmentation." Kohut did not bother to spell out—he probably took it for granted as a psychoanalytic commonplace—that the perverse sexual act "restores narcissistic equilibrium" (to revert to the vocabulary of his writings) by way of magical ideation. In other words, the pervert may consciously or unconsciously believe that through fellatio or anal intercourse it is possible to incorporate some desirable qualities (for instance masculinity) possessed by the sexual partner.

Neither did Kohut differentiate the adaptive role of perversions from that of homosexuality; as a result, his work does not allow for homosexual relations that do not have a perverse, nongenital aim. Yet such a distinction is clearly necessary. When the homosexual analysand described above was content to have relations with his lover, he experienced positive feelings (love?) for a person appreciated for real qualities; in his campaigns of conquest at the steambaths, he made serial use of anonymous victims, as if they were pins in a bowling alley.

It would be legitimate to classify such perverse activities as fetishism, for such sexual activity amounts to making use of a mere animate tool. Fetishism is mistakenly believed by many observers to be infrequent in women because in females it generally takes the outward form of heterosexual relations. One of my female analysands would occasionally lapse into this form of perversion; she became enraged in the midst of coitus if her husband took any initiative without permission, and even if he seemed to focus on his own subjectivity instead of sole devotion to giving her pleasure. Clearly, it would be equally reasonable to look upon this pattern as a sadistic perversion—it is also quite arbitrary whether we diagnose acts of pedophilia or zoophilia as fetishistic or sadistic perversions. This is probably why Bak (1974) made the suggestion that basically all perversions amount to fetishism.

Freud (1927) came to the conclusion (based on an inadequate sample that was exclusively male) that the sexual fetish represents a fantasied maternal

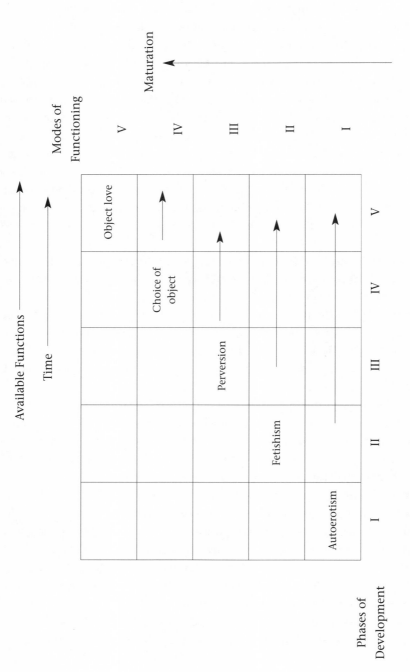

Figure 14.1. Permutations of sexuality

phallus. In my clinical experience, the fetish when used in a sexual perversion retains the magical properties that, according to Greenacre (1969), character-ize an "infantile fetish." The fantasied phallus of the mother is only one among many possible forms it may take. The sexual fetish magically satisfies a wish for omnipotent control over the milieu; hence its adaptive function is to ward off any threat of helplessness.[5] It therefore should be possible to differentiate fetishism from the other perversions on a *functional* basis (which can only be discerned on the grounds of psychoanalytic observations). Fetishism is not merely a response to narcissistic injury and depleted self-esteem; it is an anti-dote to the more drastic danger of traumatization.

This differentiation suggests that the various permutations of sexuality are best understood by means of a hierarchical developmental schema: the choice of a sexual object depends on the outcome of a later phase of development (the oedipal crisis) than do the perversions, in which sexuality is recruited to remedy difficulties in self-esteem regulation, that is, derivatives of a preoedi-pal phase wherein the self-organization is already stable. Fetishism is referable to derivatives of an even earlier phase, when no such stability has as yet been established (fig. 14.1).

Sexuality and Attachment

In parallel with the possible recruitment of sexuality to serve nonsexual adaptive ends of a remedial sort, it is also the royal road (to echo Freud) to the formation of stable human attachments. The attachment motivations of adults are buttressed by the satisfaction of their sexual motivations—as they are re-inforced by the fulfillment of needs of every kind. Thus, beyond its reproduc-tive function, sexuality is the cement of love relations. Conversely, a sexual mismatch will generally disrupt a love relationship, and sexual attraction is usually dispelled whenever the lovers' attachment fails to endure. Two indi-viduals similarly committed to asceticism (for instance, as a matter of religious conviction) may be able to perpetuate a loving bond, but if only one partner favors an asexual existence, trouble inevitably follows.

Nonetheless, infidelity is less likely to be a function of sexual difficulties in a relationship than of some problem in attachment, for instance, disillusion-ment with the partner, the emergence of some kind of hidden competitiveness, or a fear of intimacy because it is seen as a threat to autonomy. It may also con-stitute revenge for a variety of wrongs, sexual or nonsexual.

In terms of the hierarchic development of sexuality, the capacity to form lasting sexual bonds constitutes a postoedipal achievement (as I have indicated in fig. 14.1). This stage is generally reached only after adolescence.

Autoerotism

Freud (1914b) postulated that sexuality early in its maturation was not directed toward any object; he named this stage *autoerotic*, which has led to some confusion because often masturbation is also called autoerotism. Freud had in mind an intrapsychic state, not some overt behavior. In his vocabulary, masturbation may be autoerotic, or it may be accompanied by fantasies that involve a sexual partner or even a fetish. It is autoerotic if the masturbator is focused exclusively on him- or herself—not so much in the sense of self-love but as a matter of attention to the functioning of the sexual apparatus, as in the self-explorations of young children.

In the hierarchical model of sexual functions, this phase represents bedrock (fig. 14.1).

Summary

Although sexuality is clearly a biological phenomenon, there is no consensus about the relative contributions of nature and nurture to its various permutations. We still do not know the determinants of sexual excitement or to what degree this can be a response to fantasies alone. Homosexual object choice is, in part, constitutionally determined, but such predispositions are usually complemented by vicissitudes of the oedipal crisis that produce typical transference responses to the other sex. Perversions are best understood as the use of sexuality for nonerotic aims. Frequently, these aims are found to be the attempted repair of injuries to self-esteem. When perverse activities make use of a sexual partner as a mere animate tool, the transaction is classified as fetishism, albeit the overt activity may be described as one of the other perversions.

The various permutations of sexuality may be correlated with the hierarchical conception of behavior regulation.

Part III / Biological Hypotheses about Behavior and Psychoanalytic Treatment

CHAPTER FIFTEEN

The Regulation of Behavior

In part 2, I survey the essential components of a psychoanalytic theory of mind. This overview of the issues vital for a coherent, sparse, but nonreductionistic theory of mental functions is everywhere based on biology: it avoids the use of mere metaphors and of "purely psychological" notions divorced from physiology. Because each major issue is discussed more or less in isolation from the others, it remains to be shown how they are interrelated to form a comprehensive conceptualization of behavior regulation.

In a previous publication on the requirements of such a theory (Gedo 1991c), I postulated that the most economical way to construct one is to build it in accord with an epigenetic view of development that yields a hierarchical map of sequentially acquired modes of behavioral organization. As outlined in chapter 5, the development of the regulation of behavior is a direct derivative of the maturation of the central nervous system, particularly of the functions of cognition, affectivity, and semiosis (see fig. 5.1). Epigenesis means that early acquired functional capacities are not lost when superseded by more mature ones; whenever it is adaptively advantageous, the individual may temporarily make use of the earlier mode—a process called regression.

The Epigenesis of Behavior Regulation

Major changes in the functional organization of the brain also constitute nodal points in behavior regulation—times of transition from the predominance of one mode to that of its successor. Insofar as experiential factors play a role in the acquisition of vital adaptive skills in a particular phase of development (thereby structuring the brain in specific ways), the maturational challenge of that phase is met to a lesser or greater degree. Any failure to achieve autonomous competence in these basic requirements for adaptation predisposes one to functional difficulties of specific kinds whenever called upon to fend for oneself. (The typical challenge of each phase and the kind of psychopathology caused by the failure to meet it are diagrammed in figure 5.2).

In neurophysiological terms, these developmental problems lead to a variety of apraxias.

In infancy, learning takes place exclusively through "procedural memory," which does not involve cortical registration. The affectomotor schemata thus remembered therefore remain unconscious in perpetuity. If the child's milieu remains reasonably predictable, these schemata become generalized and form the basic microstructure of the personality. To transform initially passively endured experiences into psychological skills, the infant should have opportunities to practice actively reproducing those experiences; consequently, optimal development requires a balance between the involvement of a caretaker and solitary activity.

The inborn biological equipment of the newborn includes a set of constitutionally determined motivations: at a minimum, those of seeking physiological equilibria, attachment/aversion, exploration/assertion, and sensuality. As discussed in chapter 6, these motivations are not drives seeking discharge but potential patterns of response to appropriate stimuli. They operate unconsciously and automatically until the brain centers for pain and pleasure come on line. Thereafter, they tend to be actively selected to favor pleasurable and to avoid painful consequences.

Later during the first year of life, a variety of basic affects—patterned nervous system responses with subjectively experienced consequences—also become operative, in a predetermined sequence (see chap. 9). The development of an affective repertoire provides a qualitative dimension for the consequences of pursuing various motivations in given circumstances. As a result, the infant can gradually develop lasting preferences that begin to organize its behavioral tendencies—provided, of course, that its environment remains stable enough to provide reliable feedback to its behavior.

The most difficult challenge that should be mastered during the first years of life is the acquisition of increasingly autonomous competence in tension regulation. This means having the ability to avoid excessive stimulation (that would ultimately produce trauma) and the lack of stimulation (that leads to apathy). Obviously, these capacities are only acquired gradually, but, insofar as the child is in a position to influence how much stimulation it is exposed to, it should learn as early as possible to take action to keep it within some optimal range.

The various developments thus far outlined combine to produce a first (probably cerebellar) map of self-in-the-world. The first major nodal point in development occurs when maturation of the right cerebral hemisphere makes possible the beginnings of cybernetic behavioral control through the signaling function of affectivity. The earliest instance of this is the "ninth month" anxiety that impels the child to avoid what is unfamiliar—a capacity that serves to stabilize the child's exposure to novelty and thus to facilitate self-organization. Next in this sequence is the occurrence of shame stimulated by the caretaker's disapproval; this affect then serves as one guide for future conduct and eventually helps to differentiate actions that conform to the familiar self from those that do not. (These issues were more fully discussed in chapter 6.)

The major challenge of this second phase of development (roughly coincident with the second year of life) is the consolidation of a stable set of priorities for behavior, guided by the usual affective consequences of particular behavioral choices. This challenge may defeat the child if the responses of its caretakers are too unreliable—for instance, if various participants in its upbringing give irreconcilably different feedback to its activities. Such contingencies usually lead to the persistence of two or more "nuclei of the self" (Gedo and Goldberg 1973). The same outcome may result from repeated traumatization if the vulnerable "true self" becomes disavowed in the course of later development.

The achievement of (more or less complete) self-organization produces a condition wherein a basic set of affective events characterizes the subjective self. The need to keep reproducing this leitmotif of identity gives rise to behaviors Freud (1920) named "repetition compulsion." As Modell (1993) has stated, the need to affirm self-organization in this manner is a basic biological need. Hadley (2000) has postulated that this autonomous self-system is maintained by well-defined neural networks. The system may be gradually modified, but only through the repetitive experience and tolerable quanta of novelty. This is the biological given that limits the pace of fundamental personality change, in or out of treatment.

The consolidation of self-organization generally takes place amid the toddler's increasing competence in verbal communication and symbolization in general—that is, the growing dominance of the left cerebral hemisphere. Self-awareness thenceforth becomes reflective, so that the child is able to judge the value on his or her performance as well as those of the caretakers. Moreover, as a result of maturation of semantic memory, the youngster becomes more and more able to apprehend the caretakers' valuation of the child *over time*, instead of responding exclusively in the present to signs of approval or disapproval. Hence this third major phase of development largely revolves around the issue of self-esteem. Cognitively, the child begins to learn the standards of adequacy used within the family (and eventually by the wider community) and whether he or she can meet these. It is much more difficult, however, to reach similar reality-based assessments of the parents' performance, so idealization of the caretakers tends to persist into later phases of childhood.

Children who judge themselves to be inadequate (either because of unfavorable parental feedback or because of undeniable constitutional handicaps) may escape the dysphoria characteristic of this "true self" by developing a "false self" characterized by unrealistic grandiose fantasies (Kohut 1971). As children's ability to test reality improves, such illusions may be relinquished; if, however, life without illusion is too painful, the grandiosity may persist but simply be disavowed. (This process and its neurophysiological correlates are described in chap. 8.) An even more pathogenic alternative is disavowal of the primary handicaps, not through mere fantasy, but by enlisting a willing symbiotic partner (usually, of course, a parent)—to become what the novelist Joseph Conrad named a "secret sharer."[1]

Through this developmental phase, the child gradually learns to generalize parental responses to specific behaviors into a code of values. If the caretakers have not been too disillusioning (as were those of the boy described in chap. 14 who therefore made a pact with the Devil), children accept these parental codes and begin to use them to judge their own actions. This is the maturational advance Freud (1923) called superego formation. One vital consequence of the acceptance of such ideals is that thenceforth, to avoid self-condemnation, it is not sufficient to disavow the significance of unacceptable wishes. (This development is also the result of better connections among the various modules of the central nervous system.) To avoid shame and guilt, it now becomes necessary to exclude such wishes from consciousness—a defensive process called repression (see chap. 8).

An internalized conscience creates for the child the intrapsychic conflicts Freud named the Oedipus complex, because the unacceptable wishes of children at the ages of around three to six tend to involve aggression toward family members. These conflicts optimally are resolved through renunciation of childish egocentricity. Of course, this is unlikely to be accomplished if the outcome of earlier developmental crises has left the child with a legacy of narcissistic pathology. Mere repression of oedipal conflicts leads to the neurotic syndromes characterized by inhibitions, symptoms of symbolic import, and anxiety (Freud 1926).

Neither psychological development nor the maturation of the brain is completed at the close of the oedipal period. Subsequent phases have received relatively less attention within psychoanalytic theory because the outcome of these later crises cannot be correlated with typical forms of maladaptation such as those produced by the four early phases described above. These unfavorable adaptive developments are charted in figure 15.1.

Behavior Regulation in Adulthood

In adult life, derivatives of all previous developmental phases are potentially available to enhance adaptive behavior in specific circumstances, but in an "average expectable environment" (Hartmann 1939) optimal adaptation implies that the postoedipal mode of behavior regulation generally predominates. This mode includes the ability to resolve intrapsychic conflicts by setting priorities or, lacking such resolution, to tolerate the discomfort of ambivalence without defensively losing sight of either wish or countermotive. It means that self-esteem is maintained because the individual has come to terms with personal limitations and need not resort to illusions of grandiosity or unrealistic idealizations of others. A fortiori, self-organization is intact and does not require costly self-damaging enactments for its maintenance; affect and tension regulation are adequate.

Such a state of optimal adaptation cannot be maintained at all times because the milieu continually presents new challenges and exceptional stresses. For instance, unprecedented success may face an individual with a sudden triumph over competitors that mobilizes oedipal guilt; the most economical adaptive measure at such a time may be the repression of schadenfreude, of joy at the discomfort of others. Conversely, a serious defeat may mobilize aggression that, in the short run, might also best be repressed. Such possibilities of sudden, unmanageable conflict are endless.

Clinically, one can often observe unexpected disturbances of the narcissistic equilibrium of reasonably well-adapted people. One commonly used emergency response is resort to perverse sexual enactments or homosexual behaviors. There may be resort to magical fantasies, with risk taking (such as gambling or speeding) as a consequence. Others, instead of seeking compensatory grandiosity, will turn for comfort to idealized entities, sometimes human beings, more often transcendental ones. Catastrophic events may threaten the integrity of almost anyone's personality—the consequent disruption is the very

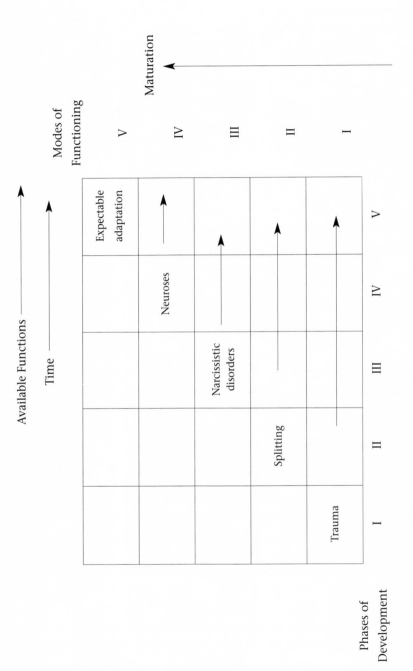

Figure 15.1. A hierarchy of pathologies

purpose of the dehumanizing cruelty inflicted on the victims of tyrannies. Traumatization may have to be avoided by total depersonalization: "This victim is not myself."[2]

All of the emergency measures I have described (and countless others that may serve the same adaptive ends) usually cease if the external stress is relieved, either spontaneously or through appropriate efforts of the affected person. Recovery may be conceptualized as the reversal of a regression that served an adaptive purpose; hence such regression can be classified as "functional" (Gedo and Goldberg 1973).

So much for the adaptive vicissitudes of reasonably healthy people. If I may use an architectural metaphor, they are like structures on solid foundations whose upper stories may yet be damaged by the winds of adversity. In contrast, personality disorders are like weak structures that buckle under the weight of the further structures that have to be built upon them. Earlier structuralizations are more fundamental than later ones; in other words, less than satisfactory outcomes of the earliest adaptive crises produce the most severe difficulties— in large measure because they compromise the individual's ability to meet the challenge of later developmental crises. How can any difficulty be overcome without adequate tension regulation? Can one attain real self-esteem if one's true self remains disavowed? And so on.

As I stated in chapter 5, the adaptive handicaps acquired in the early phases of development may interfere with later development to such an extent that only functions that mature more or less independently of other considerations remain unaffected. Such an arrest of development involving multiple functions necessitates reliance on a symbiotic partner—a condition that is difficult to meet in adulthood. If the apraxia is more focal, development may proceed through all the usual phases, provided that a variety of defensive measures remain operative—for instance, splitting off the vulnerable true self, disavowal of narcissistic injuries, or repression of intrapsychic conflicts.

The personality disturbances produced by maldevelopment in the early phases of childhood tend to be chronic, unlike acute functional regressions that may be reversed as soon as the stress that set them off has passed. (Consequently, in the analytic situation, one may observe a chronic arrest of development; rapid shifts from one functional mode to another also will occur in response to the vicissitudes of the therapeutic transaction.)

Until relatively recently, psychoanalysts generally recommended analysis only for prospective patients without obvious "preoedipal" difficulties. Clinical experience gradually convinced most practitioners that an "intact ego" (allegedly characteristic of these properly selected analysands) is almost always a theoretical fiction (Eissler 1953). In rare instances, the failure to resolve the conflicts of the Oedipus complex may be the result of some unexpected misfortune in the midst of this developmental crisis—let us say a death in the family or the incapacitation of a parent. In the great majority of cases, however, children cannot cope with these conflicts because of previously acquired handicaps such as affect intolerance, narcissistic vulnerability, magical thinking, fixation within a symbiotic adaptation, and so on. The analysand described in chapter 4 optimally illustrates this point; she could not transcend her oedipal fantasies as long as she unconsciously believed in her omnipotence. In other words, poorly resolved preoedipal issues left her unprepared to deal adaptively with the Oedipus complex.

Until about 1970, it was widely assumed that narcissistic character traits were generally caused by a regression during the oedipal period in order to avoid the anxieties stirred up by its conflicts. It was Kohut (1968, 1971) who persuasively showed that such narcissistic problems often stem from preoedipal sources—albeit occasionally their etiology *is* mainly regressive (see Gedo 1975). Kohut attributed narcissistic fixations to injuries to self-esteem in the era between the acquisition of verbal competence and the formation of structured ideals. I prefer to call that period the realm of illusions because such young children do not yet understand what is humanly possible (or impossible)—hence they tend to respond to blows to self-esteem (parental neglect, depreciation, and so forth) with compensatory fantasies of grandiosity and/or denial of the caretakers' imperfections, even unrealistic idealizations. Structured dispositions of that kind handicap the individual in dealing with subsequent vicissitudes, including oedipal ones.

The handicap is more severe in cases where maldevelopment starts even earlier, resulting in incomplete or insecure self-cohesion (see Gedo 1979, chaps. 4 and 5). Adaptively, such an outcome renders the child unable to cope with the ordinary demands of life; such an individual necessarily feels inadequate so that narcissistic pathology is inevitably added to the self-cohesion disturbance. These children have to rely on symbiotic assistance until late adolescence, a need usually met by solicitous parents. Thereafter, it is more difficult to find reliable symbiotic partners ("selfobjects," in Kohut's vocabulary). Left to their own devices, these people are unable to organize their behavior and may react with panic, further regression, or even episodes of confusion and delusional thinking. Because these dire consequences are reversible (as soon as the individual's symbiotic needs are met), these syndromes are often labeled *borderline*, that is, not quite psychotic.

Summary

We have reviewed the manner in which the infant's constitutional capacities (especially motivations, affects, and memory systems) are, in the course of maturation, progressively structured into a hierarchical array of functional modes, the self-organization. Maldevelopment in each phase of the hierarchy leads to a characteristic miscarriage of behavior regulation, that is, a distinct type of psychopathology. In adult life, various circumstances may make regression to one of the earlier modes of behavior regulation more advantageous (or even necessary) for adaptive purposes. In cases of arrested development, individuals always function in accord with the earlier modes of organization.

CHAPTER SIXTEEN

Learning and Adaptation

Psychoanalytic treatment initially aimed to relieve psychogenic symptoms; it took more than a generation of clinical experience to arrive at the realization that symptom removal, albeit quite feasible, is not etiologically relevant. Ferenczi and Rank (1923) were the first to state that psychoanalysis had to have higher ambitions, for symptoms tend to recur if the basic personality—what I prefer to term the self-organization—remains unaltered. Reich (1933) provided a manifesto for the necessary new therapeutics in a monograph entitled (in translation) *Character Analysis.*

During the next several decades analysts became preoccupied, particularly in North America, with the question of analyzability—that is, differentiation of those personality structures most likely to profit from an analytic technique focused on transference interpretation. Later studies (Kantrowitz et al. 1975, Kantrowitz 1987) demonstrated that such prognostic predictions were not reliable; none of the criteria of analyzability—the nature of intrapsychic conflicts, the predominant defensive operations and sources of anxiety, the status of object relations and narcissism—had a decisive influence on treatment outcome. As Levenson (1983) subsequently stated, psychoanalytic treatment constitutes a set of semiotic operations with potentially beneficial influence for reasons that are as yet unexplained—which is why the treatment results of the various competing psychoanalytic paradigms do not differ significantly.

Most of these rival schools concur about the commonsense proposition that adaptive change occurs if the analysand has learned something useful. I suspect that even the authors who imply something different—such as Balint's (1932) faith in a "new beginning" or Kohut's (1984) references to the healing power of empathy—might, in more sober moments, have conceded that they await a new beginning of learning, facilitated by empathic acceptance. The real differences of opinion concern *what* analysands need to learn.

Levenson's essential caveat reminded us that patients learn much more than psychoanalysts try to teach them, according to their preferred theories of technique. Witness the clinical transaction I reported in chapter 4: decades after the termination of the analysis, in a follow-up interview, the analysand gave me credit for her financial prosperity. She was no doubt correct, although we had never discussed the desirability of prudence in these matters. How, then, had she learned this from me? In all likelihood, in some nonverbal manner; perhaps as a result of my scrupulous attention to our financial transactions. Or the modesty of my office? Even in analysis, actions speak louder than words.

Events of this kind raise an even more fundamental question. When she started treatment, this person had a responsible position in a well-run business. How could she have managed *not* to acquire the requisite knowledge in the course of her day-to-day life? As it happens, late in the treatment, the answer became clear. Within her family it was well known that this woman resisted all external influence; as a small child, she became negativistic when, for several months, an illness made her mother unavailable. In later years, various serious vicissitudes apparently succeeded in taming her, but her compliance always remained a conscious manipulation. A loving older brother repeatedly warned her that she was like a pillow filled with down that assumes the shape of whoever sits upon it but promptly returns to its original form when the pressure eases.

Character traits of this sort constitute a severe learning disability, as do many other psychological configurations. For example, certain patients continue to adhere to disavowed illusions (or delusions) of omniscience that preclude accepting anything they do not know. Others hold everyone they encounter in contempt and therefore dismiss whatever these associates might have to offer; often these patients are fiercely loyal to an idealized figure to whom they attribute the views they favor. There are numerous other possibilities; suffice it to say that such learning blocks constitute the crux of most psychopathology because, without them, people almost always have many opportunities to learn in the course of daily life the adaptive skills they need.

From this vantage point, psychoanalytic therapeutics is a matter of overcoming learning disabilities. When this has been achieved, analysands absorb all kinds of useful knowledge, even silently, en passant. As my negativistic patient put it at such a juncture, this is a surrender to the analyst's way of doing things—"You have somehow brainwashed me" (see chap. 4). Unfortunately, we seldom know which of our manifold activities accomplished this desirable end. Psychoanalytic theories of treatment technique have had nothing to say on the subject (see, however, Gedo 1988, 211–26).

Common Therapeutic Errors

Although we know comparatively little about the reasons for our therapeutic successes, we have accumulated many rules of thumb (algorithms, as Levenson calls them) about avoiding failure. I have devoted chapter 4 to the discussion of one of the most significant—the need for accurate transference interpretation whenever transference interferes with the analytic collaboration. (Freud learned this lesson as early as 1901, when he failed in the attempt to treat an adolescent girl, "Dora" [Freud 1905c].)

In recent years, analysts have also begun to pay attention to their sins of commission, particularly to their tactless interventions that, even if they happen to be true, humiliate patients. Kohut may have exaggerated about the therapeutic necessity to avoid inflicting pain, but he was right to stress that the ambience of analysis should be empathic. If it is so, analysands tend to forgive the occasional unempathic lapse. When, in the third year of analysis, I spoke irritably to my negativistic patient about her manipulativeness, she said, "I feel you are accusing me of shirking, here in the analysis. But I am trying to do the best I can. Don't be so impatient! It's unjust. It's not easy to change. You should be gratified by the extent of my trust in you. Instead, you demand complete trust, without even loving me. Children can trust only if they feel loved." She was exactly right, and it was imperative to acknowledge this. It is important to discuss one's errors dispassionately, without remorse, making clear that analytic perfection is unattainable. It is equally important not to make unwarranted assumptions; it is much safer to acknowledge puzzlement or ignorance than to pretend one knows when only conjectures are available. Nor is it helpful to conceal one's inability to intervene cogently behind a veil of technically sanctioned silence.

At the same time, it is a serious mistake to allow patients to abuse or torture the analyst. Such enactments almost always form part of some transference development that calls for interpretation, but analysands engaged in such behavior are generally unable to hear comments to that effect as messages of urgent import. Quite often, they perpetuate the abuse by refusing to take seriously what the analyst communicates. To enable them to use interpretations, the enactment must first be stopped—a measure most effectively accomplished by an emphatic intervention charged with affect that conveys that the patient is in danger. If, in such transactions, the analyst behaves in a helpless manner, the treatment is likely eventually to be interrupted by the analysand.

The young woman who insightfully corrected my therapeutic error did not allow my inexperience to ruin her analysis in that manner. About my passivity in the face of her delinquent uncooperativeness, she said "You know, I actually resent that you don't require me to cooperate—that you don't compel me. It makes me feel that you are uninvolved. " She hit the nail on the head.

It is not my intention here to provide a comprehensive list of ways to spoil potential analytic success. I hope the examples I have used sufficiently convey that learning best takes place in an atmosphere of mutual respect and that it is constructive to demonstrate to patients how the *analyst* manages to learn matters of significance in a rational and reliable manner.

Let me return, instead, to the issue of what patients need to learn. Of course, *anything* they happen to learn is likely to be useful at some time or other, even if a particular bit of knowledge has no direct bearing on the psychopathology—for instance, some item of linguistic competence. Maladaptation will only be overcome, however, if dyspraxic behaviors acquired in the past can be corrected and apraxias can be mastered. (An example of correcting dyspraxia is the elimination of magical beliefs; that of an apraxia overcome is correction of an alexithymia.)

In certain instances, such changes may occur without the explicit identification of the problem, as a result of the analysand's adoption of the analyst's behaviors in the analytic situation. Improvements based on such identification have given rise to optimistic theories that analytic treatment works by way of internalizing a new object relationship (e.g., Summers 1994). It is unwise, however, passively to await such results, for in the majority of cases patients will not grasp that the analyst (like most people) possesses cognitive and semiotic skills that they themselves do not have. It will then be necessary to call their deficiencies to the patients' attention—a process that is quite likely to be painful. In these instances, learning is unlikely to take place by emulating the analyst; it may be a slow process that usually involves a great deal of direct instruction. (For instance, it may be necessary to *name* for the patient the affective reactions the analyst succeeds in identifying through direct observation of nonverbal behaviors, thereby gradually ameliorating an alexithymia.) The pace of such change is limited by the need to establish new neural networks before the use of the original ones can be relinquished.

Although analysands undoubtedly profit from whatever new information they acquire, adaptive change will only follow if they can broaden their repertoire of psychological skills. Freud (1914a) acknowledged as much when he stated that interpretation must be followed by a process of "working through." In the oral tradition of the profession, it has been common knowledge that the proper end point of psychoanalysis has been reached when the analysand has learned to conduct self-inquiry without outside intervention. Gardner (1983) pointed out that this condition will be reached most rapidly if, from the first, the analyst does not monopolize the task of interpreting the material but keeps challenging the patient to do so.

The skill of interpretation—that of translating a variety of other codes into discursive language—is only one of a series of operations every analysand has to master to make analytic treatment possible. All psychoanalytic schools agree about the role of free association in gaining access to the inner world. Analytic treatment usually begins with instructions about how to go about this; these are supplemented as necessary by reminders and the flagging of acts of omission. Analysands also have to learn how to communicate their emotions without assaulting the analyst with these. Learning to be a psychoanalytic patient is a complex process.

The skills people fail to acquire tend to be those that, in the normal course of development, should be learned very early in life. Incompetence in elementary aspects of adaptation is extremely humiliating, often leading to complications in the narcissistic realm. Analysands I have treated who had such handicaps had not asked their associates to instruct them because of their profound embarrassment or, even worse, because they disavowed the whole problem. Whom can we ask to teach us how to engage in a (civilized) conversation? This is one of the essential skills that analysands may pick up as a consequence of the semiotic rules of the psychoanalytic process. (The analyst may be able to hasten the acquisition of such know-how by pointing out patients' errors in this regard.)

We may wonder what sort of person who is lacking in such a skill would, at the same time, seek psychoanalytic help. In my practice, the individual worst afflicted with such a handicap was the child of two survivors of the Nazi death camps. Her father spoke only when absolutely necessary—fading into the woodwork was his survival strategy. Her mother and an older sister savagely competed for the spotlight; they did not listen to their interlocutors and used any opportunity to hold forth in an exhibitionistic manner. (Mother had seemingly survived the camps by flaunting her youthful charms.) My patient, albeit intellectually gifted, could not learn civilized ways in a household that echoed the atmosphere of the barracks at Auschwitz. What she had learned she had encountered in books, and this included the utility of psychoanalysis. I had to teach her that, in conversation, it is essential to take turns to *listen*. (It was not easy to achieve that, for at first to get her to listen to *that* communication I had to do some yelling.)

This clinical instance optimally illustrates what Eissler (1953) meant by the necessity of engaging in noninterpretive interventions with analysands who did not have what was then called an "intact ego" (that is, the adaptive skills required to engage in an ordinary psychoanalytic process). Incessant talking does not necessarily indicate that a patient is free associating. In cases of this sort (Lacan [1977] called them "empty speech"), the flood of words must be stopped before analysis can actually start. (In his comic novel *Portnoy's Complaint*, Philip Roth satirized the helpless passivity of some analysts: following Portnoy's book-length monologue, his analyst finally interjects, "So, now vee may perhaps to begin, yes?" It promises to be difficult.) Of course, analytic patients are unlikely to produce amusing monologues; what we often encounter is interminable obsessing about trivia.

Patients are most likely to learn psychological skills in the analytic setting in the context of a positive transference, particularly so if this involves idealization of the analyst. (Such an identification can be carried too far; for instance, it is not desirable for analysands to go around making interpretations to their associates.) It is a major technical error to attempt to instruct patients if the transference is predominantly negative, for they are likely to misinterpret what is intended as helpfulness as if it were a put-down. If the intervention involves some dangerous plan the patient is contemplating, the analyst is confronted with a choice of evils.

Correcting Dyspraxias

Other things being equal, the task of correcting dyspraxias is even more complicated than that of helping patients to acquire some bit of know-how, particularly if the patient is unaware of the maladaptive nature of the behavior in question. One form of dyspraxia has been given periodic attention in the psychoanalytic literature—namely, the avoidances that transform anxiety-laden situations into phobias. Analytic experience with phobic patients has gradually revealed that, as long as anxiety is forestalled by way of such avoidances, nothing can be discerned about the meaning of the symptoms. Adequate adaptation requires that unexplained anxieties be mastered through repeatedly going through the feared transactions. Yet it may be very difficult to convince patients who have always dealt with the unfamiliar by avoidance that getting well depends on abandoning that dyspraxic strategy. (Insisting on undergoing the expectable displeasure may needlessly evoke strong negative transferences.) There has been wide consensus among clinicians that good results depend on active efforts by these patients to stop exercising their avoidant behaviors.

Despite these pragmatic conclusions, most theories of analytic technique have failed to apply these lessons to other varieties of dyspraxia. Gill (1995) did recently state that ego syntonic behaviors that are maladaptive have to be brought to the attention of analysands in order to mobilize them to explore their significance. In my experience, the significance of most of these dyspraxic behaviors is almost self-evident: thus, avoidances deter short-term unpleasure. The problem is not that it is difficult to discern their function but that the analysand is reluctant to come to the realization that these ways are counterproductive.

Take, for example, the young woman whose parents survived the worst horrors of the Holocaust. She was scandalized by her mother's exhibitionism and greatly admired her father's low-key reaction to his past sufferings. She tried to emulate what she believed to be his patient acceptance of the fate God decreed for him. Consequently, she passively endured being abused by employers, boyfriends, and so on, in the conviction that she was thereby being virtuous. Much of this became clear early in the analysis, but nothing about it changed until the patient realized that she was quite wrong about her father. He saw *no* virtue in suffering patiently—he merely wasted no energy in fruitless complaints or protests. He was an admirable person, indeed, because of his prudence and realism. Once the patient corrected her false belief about him, she could begin the process of constructing a new set of ideals. (This is the kind of cognitive error Joseph Weiss has called a "pathogenic belief" [Weiss and Sampson et al. 1986].)

Summary

That a person's psychopathology has not been corrected as a result of the experience of ordinary living betrays the operation of some learning disability. Psychoanalysis can provide a new beginning if it overcomes such learning blocks, but we are as yet ignorant about how this is accomplished in successful cases. It is, however, clear that a positive transference enables patients usefully to identify with discrete aspects of the analyst's repertory of behavioral skills. In most cases, negative transferences and/or pathogenic beliefs must be overcome to make such desirable developments possible. Psychoanalysts have, over time, learned what must be avoided to achieve good results—errors such as humiliating patients or allowing them to be abusive or delinquent. It is often necessary to make patients confront their dyspraxic behaviors, however painful such acknowledgment may be.

CHAPTER SEVENTEEN

The Psychoanalytic Process

Once it was understood that psychoanalysis has to aim for personality change, it gradually became clear as well that, in successful instances, the treatment proceeds with an internal logic of its own. By the time the process reaches its end point, the whole sequence of the development of the analysand's personality will have become understandable. In chapter 4, I provide an example of the manner in which a legacy of narcissistic injuries at an earlier stage made impossible the resolution of one patient's oedipal crisis—a clarification of one segment of development that may serve as an excerpt from the reconstruction of the entire sequence.

In accord with the long prevalent focus of psychoanalysts on mental contents, the treatment process was usually conceived as a series of predominant transferences—predominant because in vivo they are generally present concurrently, but only the one invested with the most intense emotion at the moment is usually discerned by the analytic observer. The actualities of the analysand's life situation may determine which of the potential transference reactions will first emerge. Various intercurrent events in the course of the analysis will similarly evoke the transference with the greatest relevance in that specific situation—let us say a death in the family, a pregnancy, a love affair, a professional failure, and so on.

If no extrinsic factor of this kind is in play, the nature of the transference will most likely be determined by the analyst's technical approach. The slight differences in technique taught within the various schools of psychoanalysis do tilt the nature of the material produced by their patients in directions that legitimately lead to the theoretical propositions favored by each school. No broadly accepted analytic theory has been snatched out of thin air, but none of the competing sets of propositions is applicable to the data produced by the technical procedures of its rivals.

Analytic Corrigenda

From a biological viewpoint, the transference potentialities of analysands are epiphenomena, at least as far as their apraxic and dyspraxic disabilities are concerned. The crucial data observable in the analytic situation pertain to the predominant organizational mode by means of which patients attempt optimally to adapt, within their current capabilities, to the challenge of various circumstances (see fig. 5.2 for the modes characteristic for successive stages of development). Over lengthy periods of observation (many months, if not years), it can be determined which modes are within an analysand's repertory—that is, how far development has progressed altogether and how far, in expectable life situations, regression will proceed. (For detailed discussion of three illustrative cases, presented at some length, see Gedo 1993a, chaps. 4–9).

Because meeting the challenge of later developmental crises depends on acquiring the requisite psychological skills during earlier phases of development, we may expect that in treatment repair of the defects in a patient's adaptive repertory depends on success in addressing the maladaptive outcomes of the earliest phases implicated in the pathology. (In practice, the deficiencies cannot be tackled in a schematically neat sequence; they are usually dealt with in a catch-as-catch-can fashion, but changes do have to occur sequentially, beginning with the legacies of the most archaic phases.) Good adaptation in other respects requires repair of propensities for traumatization, depression, and psychosomatic breakdown. From a pragmatic viewpoint, such changes are difficult to accomplish. In my experience, patients sometimes return for additional treatment following seemingly successful analyses when unexpected (or cumulative) stresses overwhelm them and cause the recurrence of primitive reactions of that kind.

Paradoxically, psychoanalysis serves extremely well to relieve acute regressive episodes characterized by the foregoing syndromes, because—as Winnicott (1954) was the first to state—it constitutes a "holding environment." This atmosphere of safety produces powerful biological effects, akin to those of psychoactive medications, so that regressive reactions tend quickly to be reversed. Consequently, most psychoanalyses provide few opportunities to engage in remedial work with regard to the predispositions that play a role in the etiology of these syndromes. The situation is, of course, different if the analysand is mired in one of these regressive states, either at the start of treatment or subsequently.

In either case, strengthening the personality in ways that can prevent recurrence of such catastrophic vicissitudes is not a matter of symptomatic relief. (Psychoanalysis claims to differ from other therapies, pharmacological and psychological, because it should provide an approach toward etiological remediation.) What is needed, beyond the relief of suffering, is training in tension tolerance, in the ability to communicate affective reactions through consensually meaningful language, in self-awareness about avoiding needless stress, and so on.

The psychoanalytic method is more reliable as treatment for failures to achieve adequate self-organization, for various unintegrated nuclei of self generally do become engaged in the analytic process in the course of time. Reconciliation of the personal goals represented by these fragments of the personality into a single set of priorities—a process I call *unification* (Gedo and Goldberg 1973)—is the most urgent therapeutic task. This assertion is supported by a clinical report published by Arnold Modell (1992), a distinguished contributor to the analytic literature on therapeutic issues.

In the initial phase of the analysis, a negative transference predominated, as the patient experienced the analyst as the source of all unacceptable attitudes. She felt in danger of being deprived of her individuality by the analyst's alleged octopus-like invasiveness. She had to safeguard her private self through the process of splitting it off, leaving an inauthentic, shallow, false self to interact with the threatening other. (Modell termed this defense a schizoid withdrawal.) The analysand felt potentially humiliated by the possibility that her psychological state could be detected by others, particularly because her authentic self was generally inaccessible to herself.

Modell's therapeutic activity focused on consolidating the analysand's self-organization by countering the disavowal of those aspects of her motivations that she attributed to the analyst in the transference. In other words, he concentrated his efforts on the most archaic among the manifestations he observed. Unification of the self was accomplished when the patient was able to "own" the gamut of her motivations. Thereupon, analytic attention turned to the analysand's fear of being forced into psychic merger with potentially intrusive caretakers. Actually, the *temptation* to fall into such a symbiosis was the source of the chronic humiliation that constituted the etiology of the patient's narcissistic problems. In my judgment, however, the patient's pathology about self-esteem was a secondary complication; her primary difficulty in adaptation was caused by her "self-cohesion disturbance" (Gedo 1979).[1]

Of course, narcissistic disturbances are not always caused by poor resolution of the developmental challenges of the earliest phases of psychic life—they can just as easily result from stressful transactions in the era following the acquisition of symbolic capacities. The analysand whose treatment I most frequently use to illustrate my contentions in this book was such a person. Her experiences in the first two years of life were relatively fortunate; she was, however, severely traumatized by a lengthy separation from her mother (caused by the latter's sudden incapacitation) when she was about two years old. Precisely because this highly endowed child was, at that age, able to think in terms of concepts, she understood the absence of mother as an act of depreciation. She then reacted to this putative judgment—clearly not shared by her other caretakers—with endless rageful defiance. This included a secret megalomania through which she attempted to trump the assault on her self-esteem. In adult life, only a few manifestations of this remained conscious, such as the feeling that she never needed anybody or a sense of infinite sexual power. "It's as if I were walking through a sea of mud in a white dress; when I come out at the other end, the dress is still white. Nothing touches me . . . If anybody criticized me in the slightest, I'd drop them."

At the same time, a disavowed sense of worthlessness could abruptly surface. "I am just an insect on a pin! You put me there! I'd like to see you destroy yourself! [Like her father.] I feel defiant! I am not going to talk—you can't order me around!" Later in that same session: "I am afraid to be angry with you—it might make me lose you like I lost Daddy. I hated him because I felt belittled by him . . . When someone leaves me, I die. Separation is death, unless I do the leaving." She then had a dream about a "golden bug": "It was a symbol of what I would like to be—not a bad insect [a cockroach] but something valuable."

In cases such as hers, the pathology consists in persistence of the grandiose illusion as a result of the disavowal of its significance as a denial of the underlying wound to self-esteem (an insight first articulated by Kohut [1968, 1971]). This patient was able to transcend megalomania once she understood that her sense of worthlessness (that made her represent herself in countless dreams as a cockroach) was itself based on an early childhood misunderstanding: her mother's illness did not signify that she held her baby in low esteem. (On the contrary, mother was ill because she deprived herself of food so that her children would not be malnourished.) One of the last dreams discussed in this analysis dealt with having to admit that she had been mistaken about the identity of an important person. "A terrible misunderstanding has been made, but I discovered that it could be corrected."

In this instance, it proved to be relatively easy to correct a pathogenic belief, precisely because it was merely based on a cognitive mistake. In most of Kohut's examples (1971, 1977, 1984), the caretakers had actually depreciated the child; the therapeutic task involved undoing the "pseudo-idealization" (Gedo 1975) by means of which the victims of unfairness attempted to salvage an illusory bond with the victimizer(s). In such cases, the analyst has the difficult job of undermining the patient's illusions without causing excessive traumatic disruption (a process I call *optimal disillusionment* [Gedo and Goldberg 1973]). The chances of success are even smaller if the childhood depreciation was not unfair but inescapable—if one child among several falls short of reasonable expectations (for instance, through congenital illness or deformity, cognitive or perceptual defects, etc.). To be sure, such disadvantages may be outgrown or amply compensated through other accomplishments, but such favorable changes seldom alter the aching sense of inferiority acquired at the mother's knee.[2]

Whether grandiosity is remediable depends in part on the extent to which megalomania is built into the self-organization. In my experience, it is all but impossible to alter if it was reinforced by the grandiosity of a disturbed parent. For instance, one of my patients was consoled by her mother for any confrontation with her own inadequacy by claims that performance did not really matter, for they were better than others by virtue of descent from celebrated aristocrats. (It took this woman years to discover that these genealogical claims were highly suspect.) The mother was an open believer in magic, a cognitive system with which she indoctrinated her child. Such patients usually do their best to comply with the dictates of analytic rationality, but these efforts only amount to the construction of a false self. (For a discussion of the limits of psychoanalysis as therapy, see Gedo [1981, chap. 3; 1991, chap. 10].) Retrospectively, analysts are prone to look upon these patients as possessors of a core of psychosis—or, at the very least, as devotees of their mothers' eccentric private religions.

If a child is fortunate enough to surmount the challenge of each early developmental phase—that is, to enter the oedipal arena without significant apraxic or dyspraxic handicaps—chances are that the oedipal situation will also be mastered successfully. Of course, it is always possible that things will go radically wrong in the oedipal period, even if prior development has been optimal. For instance, one of my analysands was raised by a loving mother, while her father was absent (in the military service). The child was, in age-appropriate fashion, rivalrous with any man who was interested in her (highly attractive) mother, including her father, who returned when she was five. He responded savagely, giving the child no opportunity to develop positive feelings for him. The outcome of this crisis was a masculine identification, encouraged by the mother's cautious submissiveness to her rageful spouse. Needless to say, the child had to inhibit the aggression provoked by her father's persecution.

In addition to considerable irrational guilt—nobody ever clarified for this person that she had done no wrong—the patient came away from this situation with a nexus of additional false beliefs based on cognitive errors. She looked upon women as weak and inferior, tainted with the sin of rampant eroticism, and her reality testing was undermined by the continual triumph of falsehood within her family. The most difficult task of her analysis was to permit her to convince herself that, in fact, she could rely on her assessment of interpersonal transactions.

The Therapeutic Regression in Analysis

If a "therapeutic alliance" (Zetzel 1965) succeeds in establishing an ambience of empathy and safety (Winnicott's "holding environment"), one might intuitively predict that in the analytic situation patients would tend to function at their best and most mature. In actuality, quite the opposite generally holds true: analysands are emboldened to show their true selves (one might say, to put their worst foot forward). Defenses against the emergence of currently unacceptable, archaic aspects of the self-organization are relaxed or, in analyses conducted in accord with the most valuable aspects of so-called ego psychology (e.g., Gray 1994), rendered superfluous by means of mastery of the anxiety they were intended to ward off.

In the generation that followed Anna Freud's (1936) codification of defense mechanisms, ego psychologists emphasized that one frequently used effective defensive measure is regression to a more archaic mode of functioning, thereby avoiding oedipal anxieties. Although this proposition was illegitimately extended to the untenable generalization that the presence of archaic functional modes invariably means that such regression has taken place, it is well to remember that it is often valid. Kohut (1971) points out cogently that it is also possible to attempt the defensive maneuver of disavowing unresolved archaic issues—that is, seemingly to mature through constructing a false self. In the analytic situation, one frequently finds both types of avoidance; the analyst comes to feel that the patient is forever changing the subject.

To confront analysands with the operation of defenses and their adaptive functions is to focus on psychobiology, without regard to the specific mental contents defended against. Consistent attention to these matters will gradually reveal various aspects of the infantilism that constitutes the actual psychopathology and thus permit remedial interventions. Witness the example I used earlier in this chapter. Before this analysand was able to show either her murderous ragefulness and defiance or her tortured sense of worthlessness, she had to go through a long process of shedding the compliant facade she had built up in reaction to her father's death when she was six. This holier-than-thou surface unfavorably impressed most people who knew her well, and it was maintained at the cost of various somatizations: enuresis in latency, asthma in adolescence, out-of-wedlock pregnancies in adulthood. Here, I cannot give details about the manner in which I convinced this woman that holier-than-thou is unholy; I trust it may suffice to quote her about this after she had grasped this lesson: "I am embarrassed when I recall how ingratiating I used to be. When I had an interview at the Psychoanalytic Institute [to be accepted as a low-fee patient] I said, 'Oh, how do you do, Miss A.; I'm so glad to meet you'— so false, so cloyingly sweet."

Summary

Successful analysis has been understood as a process that consists of a succession of transferences, but the nature of these is inevitably skewed by the analyst's theoretically-based interventions. Hence it is preferable to chart analytic progress in terms of the fluctuations in the modal organization of behavior regulation.

Because the psychoanalytic situation has powerful biological effects (analogous to that of psychoactive drugs), analytic treatment often counters any tendency to regress to the most archaic levels of functioning, sometimes leading to subsequent difficulties in especially stressful situations. Actual repair of profound personality problems requires addressing the maladaptive outcomes of the earliest developmental crises, such as any failure to achieve self-cohesion, or the crystallization and disavowal of pathogenic beliefs. This is made possible by the analytic ambience of safety and empathy that permits patients to reveal their true selves.

CHAPTER EIGHTEEN

Unsolved Problems

It is widely understood that the manner in which the neurochemical activities of brain cells produce verbally encoded thoughts remains a mystery—in scientific circles, this problem is often called the "hard question." This bleak status quo until recently has discouraged the majority of psychoanalysts from attempts to embed the discipline within biology. Freud's century-old effort to do so has fallen into disuse; mentalist viewpoints now dominate the field; even purely hermeneutic theories are gaining favor.

If it is granted, however, that adaptation and the control of behavior primarily depend on the manner in which the individual deals with the contents of thought, we may conclude that *for psychoanalysis* the lack of answers to the hard question does not constitute an immediate problem. The biology of symbolic thought does not change depending upon its content, be it shoes, and ships, and sealing wax—or whether pigs have wings.

Quantitative Questions

On the other hand, there are a number of behavioral variables of physiological origin that are psychoanalytically highly pertinent but for which we still lack understanding of the causes of the variations. In my judgment, the most significant among these open questions is that of emotional intensity. Shevrin (1997) has cogently argued that variation in that regard cannot be accounted for on the basis of the prevalent affect theories, among them the theory of affects I espouse in this book. The issue of intensity did not go unaddressed in this fashion in psychoanalytic discourse as long as Freud's metapsychology held sway. In Hartmann's (1964, 155–81) version of the theory, for example, various degrees of "neutralization" were posited to explain variations in intensity. In his *Project for a Scientific Psychology* (1895a), Freud alluded to this matter in terms of "quantities of excitation."

Although we cannot maintain any longer that the concept of psychic energy is valid biologically (Holt 1967, Swanson 1977), it seems that psychoanalytic theory does need a psychoeconomic viewpoint. The mosaic of affectivity lends quality to psychic experience; some analogous biological variable must account for its quantitative dimensions. Perhaps, something similar to the sleep/wakefulness gradient may be involved—a blandness/vehemence gradient? We do not know what determines the endogenous contribution to individual variations in this regard—not even that of the changes at various times within the same person along this quantitative axis.

Another unexplained biological variable with potential clinical significance is the gradient within any population from aversion-to-change to preference-for-novelty (see Moraitis 1988). The relevance of such a characteristic for achieving improved adaptation through therapeutic intervention is almost self-evident. Moraitis pointed out that phobic avoidances are basically directed against accommodation to the unfamiliar. It is conceivable that such aspects of the self-organization are structured as a result of consistently unpleasurable experiences when the infant engaged in exploratory activities. Alternatively, the same consequences might ensue if a child is subjected to so many unassimilable changes in its overall milieu (ostensibly producing chronic confusion) that all change is thereupon experienced as potentially traumatic.

Plausible as such explanations may seem, psychoanalysts have collected no clinical evidence to support them. Even if they did hold true in certain instances, that would not rule out the equally likely possibility that constitutional factors may be more significant in producing variations along this gradient than are experiential ones.

In the chapter on affectivity, I allude to our inadequate understanding of the biology of the complex affects that arise in reaction to verbally encoded judgments about interpersonal relations. Our ignorance is compounded by the fact that we are also unable to account for the quantitative dimension of affective reactions—the degree of passion involved. As Hamlet says about an actor's tearful performance,

> . . . all for nothing! For Hecuba!
> What's Hecuba to him or he to Hecuba,
> That he should weep for her?

This is in contrast to Hamlet's own state, lacking in "gall." It is not simply a matter of demonstrativeness but one of *feeling*.

Individual Differences

Analogously, we lack any biological explanation for individual differences in the propensity for deep regression—into depression, somatization, or psychosis—as a response to various degrees of stress. Why do some people maintain their usual level of adaptation in the face of the "slings and arrows of outrageous fortune," while, in apparently similar circumstances, others collapse into archaic adaptive modes? In the latter days of the dominance of the ego psychological paradigm, we resorted to the metaphor of "ego strength" (or weakness) in discussing this question. (It was the last of the military metaphors Freud made de rigueur for psychoanalysis: "They shall not pass!") Even if we update the phrase better to conform to current usage, to talk of the integrity of self-organization versus its disruption, the basic question about individual differences remains unanswered.

Moreover, the issue goes beyond mere self-cohesion; ego strength referred to matters such as frustration tolerance, the capacity to live with grief and anxiety, and to come to terms with whatever is possible by way of renunciation: to have courage. This may partly be a matter of the person's system of ideals—but collapse may also take place in the face of the best of intentions.

We are equally ignorant about the biology of perseverance, particularly in instances that do not involve any of our inborn motivations (see chap. 6). We need to persist in pursuit of long-term goals—like finishing this book—even when such activity brings no immediate pleasure or profit. I once treated a celebrated mathematician who confided the secret of his success during an episode of positive transference: he worked harder than anyone else! This turned out to mean that he persevered with focused attention on a problem, without interruption, for as long as seventy-two hours. He had no idea that others were incapable of such persistence, even if there was a pot of gold at the end of a rainbow.

I am confident that my patient was biologically different from almost everyone else. Traditionally, this difference was ascribed to a faculty called "volition"—a philosophical concept without scientific standing. "Strength of will," albeit only a metaphor, does convey that there are individual differences in our ability to carry out our intentions in the absence of short-term rewards.

Undoubtedly, there are numerous additional questions about the biology of behavior regulation, answers to which would enhance the therapeutic potency of psychoanalysis, but I content myself here with a brief discussion of just one of these—the continuing puzzle of how psychological matters of various kinds may lead, in biologically predisposed individuals, to malfunction and even tissue pathology in particular physiological systems. This question was already raised in the nineteenth century, under the rubric of "the mysterious leap" from mind to body.

It has been understood for some time that constitutional vulnerabilities, involving multiple genes, are implicated in the etiology of schizophrenia and major depressive illness, the "psychosomatic diseases" par excellence. Under psychological stress these deficiencies produce complex neurochemical abnormalities. The latter are not as yet understood in detail. From a psychoanalytic perspective, what we most need to learn is the nature of the childhood training that will structure the central nervous system so as to protect constitutionally vulnerable infants against future psychotic breakdown. Such knowledge might be applied in prophylactic ways in the context of psychoanalytic treatment.

The biological mechanisms through which psychological stress leads to functional difficulties in systems other than the brain are still to be uncovered, so that—for the moment—all analysts can do about "psychosomatic" problems is to help patients to overcome any denial of their vulnerability to stress. This will often lead to adaptive changes that diminish stress to such an extent that the somatic malfunction is significantly relieved.[1] To do better than that, psychoanalysts have to learn how to train the central nervous system to deal with stress by means of cortical processes alone.

Last Words

The optimism of my agenda for a viable future of psychoanalysis may to some readers seem quixotic. Indeed, my program remains nothing short of grandiose as long as the traditional technique of psychoanalysis remains sacrosanct. Nor are most clinicians today ready to embrace technical changes that reduce their role from that of benign foster parents to one of physiotherapists for the brain. Sometimes this reluctance takes the guise of opposition to scientism, sometimes that of preserving our humanistic antecedents. At any rate, it betokens a sentimental view of therapeutic transactions as reflections of the best relationship possible among humans. Alas, that is more or less necessary but not sufficient.

As Gardner (1983) was the first to note, even the traditional technique of psychoanalysis works only insofar as it trains the analysand to perform effective self-inquiry. As I have previously stated (Gedo 1995a), such training can only be understood as a restructuring of the relevant portions of the central nervous system (not the cerebral cortex alone). Levenson's (1983) idea that the effectiveness of psychoanalysis depends on the rules of its semiosis points toward the same conclusion. Traditional interpretive technique continues to be useful when transference resistance becomes an obstacle to learning new ways of processing information, but mutative interventions must then follow, and these are truly analogous to the activities of physiotherapists.

If the task of the psychoanalyst is to induce analysands to acquire new psychological faculties through the exercise of hitherto neglected functions, we must also face the fact that, to do the job most effectively, we need as much information as possible about the actual physiology of behavior regulation.

Perhaps, to accept that challenge, we need a fresh cadre of clinicians, committed to psychoanalysis as a biological science. A consummation devoutly to be wished.

Notes

ONE: The Enduring Scientific Contributions of Sigmund Freud

1. Levin points out that Freud pragmatically found a way to facilitate new learning through the method of free association, which creates "learning windows" by activating working memory for the associated material by means of spontaneity (2003, 227–28).

TWO: Hermeneutics and Biology in the Psychoanalytic Situation

1. It is no coincidence that it is Brenner who has called into question the very notion of working through, for he has consistently argued against the concept of "actual neuroses" as well (see Brenner 1982). He is not interested in psychoeconomic issues—the matters designated as quantitative (Qn) in Freud's *Project*. It is surprising that a prominent ego psychologist should so radically disagree about one of the streams of clinical evidence that persuaded Freud that his 1900 topographic theory of mind was not adequate to explicate the full range of his observations, leading to the very conceptualization of "ego." (For details of these theoretical considerations, see Gedo and Goldberg 1973.)

2. Recall that Freud's original definition of transference (1900, 562–63) referred to the transfer of the intensity of an idea in the unconscious to some preconscious content (and not specifically to matters related to the analytic relationship). In his view, analytic treatment has been successful when the relationship to the analyst loses the qualities characteristic for "id" functioning.

THREE: Alternatives to Freud's Biological Theory

1. For an illuminating clinical illustration of such a sequence, based on self-observation, see Valenstein 1995.

FOUR: The Psychoanalytic Import of Mental Contents

1. Clinical illustrations throughout this book are offered merely to help readers apprehend the meaning of abstract concepts; they are nowhere intended to prove my contentions. No amount of anecdotal material can suffice to provide such proof.

2. Interpretations based on the analyst's response to a transference enactment are often characterized as "from the countertransference."

3. In the first case presented in this chapter, the analyst tried to interfere with an extraanalytic transference reaction in a psychotherapeutic manner while the analytic transference escalated into a stalemate.

FIVE: Personality Development and Psychopathology

1. Throughout this book, the conditions described will be those for right-handed individuals.

2. The principles of such a hierarchy were first enunciated about neural control by Hughlings Jackson (1884). As Grossman (1993) has shown, in his conceptual work, Freud generally followed the same principles.

3. Trauma will be discussed in greater detail in chapter 7.

4. For an account of such a problem and its attempted treatment, see Gedo 1988, 61–66.

5. For detailed discussions of a wide spectrum of more circumscribed regulatory deficits, see Gedo 1988, 91–93, 178–86.

6. For further discussion of cognitive defects, see Gedo 1988, 187–97, and chap. 12 of this volume; for disorders of communication, see Gedo 1996.

7. For an account of an analysis that illustrates the repetition compulsion and the consequences of its cessation, see Gedo 1988, 18–25, 74.

SIX: A Hierarchy of Motivations as Self-organization

1. Such fantasies are made possible by the achievement of a certain degree of symbolic competence. Psychoanalytic clinical experience suggests that childhood masturbation often begins between the ages of three and four, usually accompanied by fantasy.

2. On the issue of "merger transference," see Kohut 1971.

3. The experience concretizes the sense of imminent traumatization barely avoided.

SEVEN: Trauma and Its Vicissitudes

1. I have previously described certain episodes of her analysis in Gedo 1988, 77–79.

2. A transcript of this presentation and its discussion constitutes chapter 5 in Gedo and Gehrie 1993.

3. I have previously described this unusual case in Gedo 1988, 86–88.

4. Kohut (1971) was the first to note that frantic physical activity is designed to enhance a sense of bodily integrity.

EIGHT: Breakdowns in Information Processing

1. In a 1917 letter to G. Groddeck (in E. Freud 1960).

2. This is the condition Freud's mentor, Joseph Breuer, called a "hypnoid state" (Breuer and Freud 1895, chap. 2).

NINE: Affectivity

1. It is true that some individuals are shameless; such delinquent personalities are, however, unresponsive to vain efforts to shame them.

TEN: Dreams and Dreaming

1. It is common to observe dreaming in dogs, sometimes accompanied by some degree of organized motility on the part of the sleeping animal. One of my dogs, after he was sideswiped by a car, had a traumatic dream in the course of which he ran around in circles, howling. Nothing could better demonstrate that the dream is part of an endeavor to reprocess an unassimilated experience.

2. The verbal content of poetry is apprehended through the secondary process, the physical properties of its prosody via subsymbolic channels.

3. I made note of this dream to use in a paper published in Barron (1993).

ELEVEN: The Biopsychology of Early Experience

1. I have had no clinical experience with individuals who suffer from such conditions.

2. For detailed discussions of the question of consciousness, see Levin 2003, part 3.

3. I previously published much of this clinical material in Gedo 1988, 18–25.

TWELVE: Disorders of Thought

1. For a full report on this treatment, see Gedo 1979, chaps. 6 and 7. The excellent results of this analysis were confirmed by a follow-up some twenty-five years later.

2. A detailed presentation of this case was published in Gedo and Gehrie 1993, chap. 2.

3. Scott Dowling, in an unpublished presentation to the American Psychoanalytic Association about a dozen years ago, therefore characterized this phenomenon as "transitional," in the sense introduced by Winnicott (1951).

4. For further examples of focal defects in cognition, see Lichtenberg 1983.

THIRTEEN: Object Relations

1. Kohut's original clinical observation was valid and highly significant. Unfortunately, he died before he was able to offer a coherent theoretical explanation for it.

2. For a description of this kind of therapeutic transaction, see Gedo and Gehrie 1993, chap. 3.

3. For a full account of this analysis, see Gedo 1979, chaps. 6 and 7.

4. The rituals of almost all religions have analogous magical connotations and confer protective benefits upon the believer.

5. For a more extensive presentation of this analysis, see Gedo 1981, chaps. 1 and 9 (case 3).

FOURTEEN: Permutations of Sexuality

1. Currently, among these only pedophilia is regarded as unequivocally pathological.

2. I defer discussion of the so-called perverse sexual aims implicit in most homosexual experiences to the section on perversion that follows.

3. This sample is very small, but one person's total analytic case load is of necessity limited. Homosexuals constituted about three percent of my practice—a proportion in line with their number in the population at large.

4. Clearly, the heterosexual Don Juan is often engaging in behaviors that have the same significance. The same is true of pedophilia and zoophilia.

5. For the report of an analysis that brought to light the surprising meaning of a fetish as the representation of the mother's pregnancy, see Gedo 1981, chap. 12. By turning the clock back through such a fantasy, this patient was able to negate the catastrophic events that followed the mother's delivery.

FIFTEEN: The Regulation of Behavior

1. Kohut (1971, 1977, 1984) may have been first to stress the frequency of this kind of adaptation; he called it reliance on a "selfobject." In his system, this is looked upon as ubiquitous and well-adapted, even in adult life.

2. I learned this from the autobiographical account of a psychoanalyst who lived through Auschwitz.

SEVENTEEN: The Psychoanalytic Process

1. In his 1992 report, Modell did not discuss the childhood roots of this propensity for splitting. In my clinical experience, it generally stems from a combination of actual parental intrusiveness and the fact that, for the child, it is the symbiotic state that is familiar and therefore pleasurable and safe.

2. I do not mean to imply that the parent(s) of every defective infant inevitably react with disappointment that outweighs other reactions to the child—only that such disappointment is simply human.

EIGHTEEN: Unsolved Problems

1. For an extensive presentation of an analysis that accomplished such change, see Gedo 1984, chap. 4, especially pp. 67–69.

References

Abraham, K., S. Ferenczi, E. Jones, and E. Simmel. 1919. *Psychoanalysis and the War Neuroses*. English translation, London: International Psycho-Analytic Press, 1921.

Alexander, F., and T. French. 1946. *Psychoanalytic Therapy*. New York: Ronald Press.

Arlow, J., and C. Brenner. 1964. *Psychoanalytic Concepts of the Structural Theory*. New York: International Universities Press.

Bacon, K., and J. Gedo. 1993. Ferenczi's contributions to psychoanalysis: Essays in dialogue. In *The Legacy of Sandor Ferenczi*, ed. L. Aron and A. Harris, 121–39. Hillsdale, NJ: Analytic Press.

Bak, R. 1974. Distortions of the concept of fetishism. *Psychoanalytic Study of the Child* 29:191–214.

Balint, M. 1932. Character analysis and new beginnings. In *Primary Love and Psychoanalytic Technique*, 151–64. London: Maresfield Library, 1985.

Barron, J., ed. 1993. *Self-Analysis*. Hillsdale, NJ: Analytic Press.

Basch, M. 1976. The concept of affect: A reexamination. *Journal of the American Psychoanalytic Association* 24:759–77.

———. 1983. The perception of reality and the disavowal of meaning. *Annual of Psychoanalysis* 11:125–54.

Benedek, T. 1973. *Psychoanalytic Investigations*. New York: Quadrangle.

Bettelheim, B. 1950. *Love Is Not Enough*. Glencoe, IL: Free Press.

Bollas, C. 1987. *The Shadow of the Object*. New York: Columbia University Press.

Bowlby, J. 1969. *Attachment and Loss*. Vol. 1. New York: Basic Books.

Brenner, C. 1982. *The Mind in Conflict*. New York: International Universities Press.

———. 1987. Working Through: 1914–1984. *Psychoanalytic Quarterly* 56:88–108.

Breuer, J., and S. Freud. 1895. *Studies in Hysteria. Standard Edition*, vol. 2. London: Hogarth Press, 1955.

Bucci, W. 1993. The development of emotional meaning in free association: A multiple code theory. In *Hierarchical Concepts in Psychoanalysis*, ed. A. Wilson and J. Gedo, 3–47. New York: Guilford.

———. 1997. *Psychoanalysis and Cognitive Science*. New York: Guilford.

Damasio, A. 1994. *Descartes' Error: Emotion, Reason and the Human Brain*. London: Macmillan.

———. 1997. *Psychoanalysis and Cognitive Science*. New York: Guilford.

Dorpat, T., and M. Miller. 1992. *Clinical Interaction and the Analysis of Meaning.* Hillsdale, NJ: Analytic Press.

Eissler, K. 1953. The effect of the structure of the ego on psychoanalytic technique. *Journal of the American Psychoanalytic Association* 1:104–43.

Ekman, P. 1992. An argument for basic emotions. *Cognition and Emotion* 6, no. 3–4: 169–200.

Ekman, P., and R. Davidson, eds. 1994. *The Nature of Emotion: Fundamental Questions.* Oxford: Oxford University Press.

Fairbairn, W. 1954. *An Object Relations Theory of Personality.* New York: Basic Books.

Ferenczi, S. 1912. On transitory symptom-constructions during the analysis. In *Contributions to Psychoanalysis*, 2d ed., retitled *Sex in Psychoanalysis*, 154–86. New York: Dover, 1956.

———. 1928. The elasticity of psychoanalytic technique. In *Final Contributions to the Problems and Methods of Psychoanalysis*, 87–101. New York: Brunner/Maazel, 1980.

———. 1931. Child analysis in the analyses of adults. In *Final Contributions to the Problems and Methods of Psychoanalysis*, 126–42. New York: Brunner/Maazel, 1980.

Ferenczi, S., and O. Rank. 1923. *The Development of Psycho-analysis.* Reprint, New York: Dover, 1956.

Fonagy, P., G. Gergely, E. Jurist, and M. Target. 2002. *Affect Regulation, Mentalization, and the Development of the Self.* New York: Other Press.

Frank, A. 1969. The unrememberable and the unforgettable: Passive primal repression. *Psychoanalytic Study of the Child* 24:59–66.

Freedman, D. 1997. *On Infancy and Toddlerhood.* Madison, CT: International Universities Press.

French, T. 1952. *The Integration of Behavior.* Vol. 1. Chicago: University of Chicago Press.

Freud, A. 1936. *The Ego and the Mechanisms of Defense.* First English ed., New York: International Universities Press, 1946.

———. 1965. *Normality and Pathology in Childhood.* New York: International Universities Press.

Freud, E., ed. 1960. *The Letters of Sigmund Freud, 1875–1939.* New York: Basic Books.

Freud, S. 1886–1957. *The Standard Edition of the Complete Psychological Works of Sigmund Freud.* 24 vols. Ed. J. Strachey. London: Hogarth Press, 1953–1966.

———. 1892. Sketches for the "preliminary communication" of 1893. *Standard Edition*, 1:147–56. London: Hogarth Press, 1966.

———. 1893. On the psychical mechanism of hysterical phenomena. *Standard Edition*, 3:26–42. London: Hogarth Press, 1962.

———. 1894. The neuro-psychoses of defense. *Standard Edition*, 3:45–61. London: Hogarth Press, 1962.

———. 1895a. Project for a scientific psychology. *Standard Edition*, 1:295–391. London: Hogarth Press, 1966.

———. 1895b. A reply to criticism of my paper on anxiety neurosis. *Standard Edition*, 3:121–41. London: Hogarth Press, 1962.

———. 1895c. On the grounds for detaching a particular syndrome from neurasthenia under the description "anxiety neuroses." *Standard Edition*, 3:87–120. London: Hogarth Press, 1962.

———. 1896a. Further remarks on the neuropsychoses of defence. *Standard Edition*, 3:159–88. London: Hogarth Press, 1962.

———. 1896b. The aetiology of hysteria. *Standard Edition*, 3:189–224. London: Hogarth Press, 1962.

———. 1898. Sexuality in the aetiology of the neuroses. *Standard Edition*, 3:261–87. London: Hogarth Press, 1962.

———. 1900. *The Interpretation of Dreams. Standard Edition*, vols. 4 and 5. London: Hogarth Press, 1955.

———. 1901. *The Psychopathology of Everyday Life. Standard Edition*, vol. 6. London: Hogarth Press, 1960.

———. 1905a. *Jokes and their Relation to the Unconscious. Standard Edition*, vol. 8. London: Hogarth Press, 1960.

———. 1905b. Three essays on the theory of sexuality. *Standard Edition*, 7:136–248. London: Hogarth Press, 1955.

———. 1905c. Fragment of an analysis of a case of hysteria. *Standard Edition*, 7:3–122. London: Hogarth Press, 1953.

———. 1909a. Analysis of a phobia in a five year old boy. *Standard Edition*, 10:3–147. London: Hogarth Press, 1955.

———. 1909b. Notes upon a case of obsessional neurosis. *Standard Edition*, 10:153–250. London: Hogarth Press, 1955.

———. 1911a. Formulations of the two principles of mental functioning. *Standard Edition*, 12:215–28. London: Hogarth Press, 1958.

———. 1911b. Psycho-analytic notes on an autobiographical account of a case of paranoia (Dementia paranoides). *Standard Edition*, 12:3–84. London: Hogarth Press, 1958.

———. 1911–1915. Papers on technique. *Standard Edition*, 12:89–174. London: Hogarth Press, 1958.

———. 1912. The dynamics of transference. *Standard Edition*, 12:97–108. London: Hogarth Press, 1958.

———. 1914a. Remembering, repeating, and working through. *Standard Edition*, 12:146–56. London: Hogarth Press, 1958.

———. 1914b. On narcissism: An introduction. *Standard Edition*, 14:73–102. London: Hogarth Press, 1957.

———. 1915a. Observations on transference love. *Standard Edition*, 12:158–74. London: Hogarth Press, 1958.

———. 1915b. The unconscious. *Standard Edition*, 14:166–204. London: Hogarth Press, 1957.

———. 1915c. Repression. *Standard Edition*, 14:146–58. London: Hogarth Press, 1958.

———. 1916. Some character-types met with in psychoanalytic work. *Standard Edition*, 14:311–36. London: Hogarth Press, 1957.

———. 1916–17. *Introductory Lectures on Psycho-Analysis. Standard Edition*, vols. 15 and 16. London: Hogarth Press, 1963.

———. 1918. From the history of an infantile neurosis. *Standard Edition*, 17:7–124. London: Hogarth Press, 1955.

———. 1920. Beyond the pleasure principle. *Standard Edition*, 18:3–64. London: Hogarth Press, 1955.

———. 1923. The ego and the id. *Standard Edition*, 19:3–66. London: Hogarth Press, 1961.

———. 1926. Inhibitions, symptoms, and anxiety. *Standard Edition*, 20:87–172. London: Hogarth Press, 1959.

———. 1927. Fetishism. *Standard Edition*, 21:149–57. London: Hogarth Press, 1961.

————. 1933. New introductory lectures on psycho-analysis. *Standard Edition*, 22:3–182. London: Hogarth Press, 1964.

————. 1937. Constructions in analysis. *Standard Edition*, 23:255–70. London: Hogarth Press, 1964.

————. 1940. An outline of psycho-analysis. *Standard Edition*, 23:141–207. London: Hogarth Press, 1964.

Friedman, G. 1991. Perspectives on the analytic stalemate: Case presentation. *Contemporary Psychoanalysis* 27:483–93.

Gardner, R. 1983. *Self-Inquiry.* Hillsdale, NJ: Analytic Press, 1989.

Gedo, J. 1975. Forms of idealization in the analytic transference. *Journal of the American Psychoanalytic Association* 23:485–505.

————. 1979. *Beyond Interpretation.* New York: International Universities Press.

————. 1981. *Advances in Clinical Psychoanalysis.* New York: International Universities Press.

————. 1984. *Psychoanalysis and its Discontents.* New York: Guilford.

————. 1986. *Conceptual Issues in Psychoanalysis.* Hillsdale, NJ: Analytic Press.

————. 1988. *The Mind in Disorder.* Hillsdale, NJ: Analytic Press.

————. 1991a. *The Biology of Clinical Encounters.* Hillsdale, NJ: Analytic Press.

————. 1991b. The analytic stalemate: Discussion. *Contemporary Psychoanalysis* 27: 502–11.

————. 1991c. Between prolixity and reductionism: Psychoanalytic theory and Occam's razor. *Journal of the American Psychoanalytic Association* 39:71–86.

————. 1992. Discussion of Arnold Modell's "The private self and private space." *Annual of Psychoanalysis* 20:15–24. Hillsdale, NJ: Analytic Press.

————. 1993a. *Beyond Interpretation.* Rev. ed. Hillsdale, NJ: Analytic Press.

————. 1993b. Empathy, new beginnings, and analytic cure. *Psychoanalytic Review* 80:507–18.

————. 1995a. Working through as metaphor and as a modality of treatment. *Journal of the American Psychoanalytic Association* 43:339–56.

————. 1995b. Encore. *Journal of the American Psychoanalytic Association* 43:384–92.

————. 1996. *The Languages of Psychoanalysis.* Hillsdale, NJ: Analytic Press.

————. 1999. *The Evolution of Psychoanalysis.* New York: Other Press.

Gedo, J., and M. Gehrie. *Impasse and Innovation in Psychoanalysis.* Hillsdale, NJ: Analytic Press.

Gedo, J., and A. Goldberg. 1973. *Models of the Mind.* Chicago: University of Chicago Press.

Gill, M. 1976. Metapsychology is not psychology. In *Psychology Versus Metapsychology,* ed. M. Gill and P. Holzman. Psychological Issues, no. 36, pp. 71–105. New York: International Universities Press, 1976.

————. 1981. The boundaries of psychoanalytic data and technique: A critique of Gedo's *Beyond Interpretation. Psychoanalytic Inquiry* 1:205–32.

————. 1995. *Psychoanalysis in Transition.* Hillsdale, NJ: Analytic Press.

Gill, M., and P. Holzman, eds. 1976. *Psychology Versus Metapsychology.* Psychological Issues, no. 36. New York: International Universities Press.

Glover, E. 1931. The therapeutic effect of inexact interpretation: A contribution to the theory of suggestion. *International Journal of Psycho-Analysis* 12:397–411.

Goldberg, A., ed. 1978. *The Psychology of the Self.* New York: International Universities Press.

Gould, S. 1995. Asking big questions on science and meaning. *New York Times*, October 16, 1995, B2.

Gray, P. 1994. *The Ego and the Analysis of Defense*. Northvale, NJ: Jason Aronson.

Greenacre, P. 1967. The influence of infantile trauma on genetic patterns. In *Emotional Growth*. New York: International Universities Press.

———. 1969. The fetish and the transitional object. *Psychoanalytic Study of the Child* 24:144–64.

Greenberg, J. 1991. *Oedipus and Beyond*. Cambridge, MA: Harvard University Press.

Greenberg, J., and S. Mitchell. 1983. *Object Relations in Psychoanalytic Theory*. Cambridge, MA: Harvard University Press.

Grossman, W. 1976. Knightmare in armor: Reflections on Wilhelm Reich's contributions to psychoanalysis. *Psychiatry* 39:376–85.

———. 1984. Freud and Horney: A study of psychoanalytic models via the analysis of a controversy. In *Psychoanalysis: The Science of Mental Conflict*, ed. A. Richards and M. Willick, 65–87. Hillsdale, NJ: Analytic Press.

———. 1993. Hierarchies, boundaries, and representation in a Freudian model of mental organization. In *Hierarchical Concepts in Psychoanalysis*, ed. A. Wilson and J. Gedo, 170–202. New York: Guilford.

Grünbaum, A. 1984. *The Foundations of Psychoanalysis*. Berkeley: University of California Press.

Guntrip, H. 1968. *Schizoid Phenomena, Object-Relations and the Self*. New York: International Universities Press.

Hadley, J. 1985. Attention, affect, and attachment. *Psychoanalysis and Contemporary Thought* 8:529–50.

———. 1989. The neurobiology of motivational systems. In J. Lichtenberg, *Psychoanalysis and Motivation*, 337–72. Hillsdale, NJ: Analytic Press.

———. 1992. The instincts revisited. *Psychoanalytic Inquiry* 12:396–418.

———. 1996. Personal letter.

———. 2000. The self-organization and the autonomy system. *Annual of Psychoanalysis* 28:67–84. Hillsdale, NJ: Analytic Press.

Harlow, H. 1962. The effect of rearing conditions on behavior. *Bulletin of the Menninger Clinic* 26:213–24.

Hartmann, H. 1939. *Ego Psychology and the Problem of Adaptation*. New York: International Universities Press, 1958.

———. 1964. *Essays in Ego Psychology*. New York: International Universities Press.

Hartmann, H., E. Kris, and R. Loewenstein. 1964. *Papers on Psychoanalytic Psychology*. Psychological Issues, no. 14. New York: International Universities Press.

Hoffman, I. 1991. Discussion: Toward a social-constructivist view of the analytic situation. *Psychoanalytic Dialogue* 1:74–105.

———. 1992. Some practical implications of a social-constructivist view of the psychoanalytic situation. *Psychoanalytic Dialogue* 2:287–304.

Holt, R. 1965. A review of some of Freud's biological assumptions and their influence on his theories. In *Psychoanalysis and Current Biological Thought*, ed. N. Greenfield and W. Lewis, 93–124. Madison: University of Wisconsin Press.

———. 1967. Beyond vitalism and mechanism: Freud's concept of psychic energy. In *Science and Psychoanalysis*, vol. 2, ed. J. Masserman, 1–41. New York: Grune and Stratton.

———. 1976. Drive or wish? A reconsideration of the psychoanalytic theory of activation. In *Psychology Versus Metapsychology*, ed. M. Gill and P. Holzman, 158–96. Psychological Issues, no. 36. New York: International Universities Press, 1976.

———. 1989. *Freud Reappraised: A Fresh Look at Psychoanalytic Theory*. New York: Guilford.

Homans, P. 1979. *Jung in Context*. Chicago: University of Chicago Press.

Hughlings Jackson, J. 1884. Evolution and dissolution of the nervous system. In *Selected Writings of Hughlings Jackson*, ed. J. Taylor. New York: Basic Books, 1958.

Izard, C. 1991. *The Psychology of Emotions*. New York: Plenum Press.

Joseph, E. 1985. Further comments on the therapeutic action of psychoanalysis. In *Psychoanalysis: The Vital Issues*, ed. G. Pollock and J. Gedo, vol. 2, 205–26. New York: International Universities Press.

Jung, C. 1963. *Memories, Dreams, Reflections*. New York: Vintage.

Kantrowitz, J. 1987. Suitability for psychoanalysis. *Yearbook of Psychoanalytic Psychotherapy* 2:403–15.

Kantrowitz, J., S. Singer, and P. Knapp. 1975. Methodology for a prospective study of psychoanalysis: The role of psychological tests. *Psychoanalytic Quarterly* 44:371–91.

Kanzer, M. 1973. Two prevalent misconceptions about Freud's "Project" (1895). *Annual of Psychoanalysis* 1:88–103.

Kernberg, O. 1976. *Object Relations Theory and Clinical Psychoanalysis*. New York: Jason Aronson.

Klein, G. 1976. *Psychoanalytic Theory*. New York: International Universities Press.

Klein, M. 1946. Notes on some schizoid mechanisms. In *Writings*, 3:1–24. New York: Free Press, 1984.

———. 1952. Some theoretical conclusions about the emotional life of the infant. In *Writings*, 3:61–93. New York: Free Press, 1984.

———. 1957. Envy and gratitude. In *Writings*, 3:176–235. New York: Free Press, 1984.

———. 1984. *The Writings of Melanie Klein*. 4 vols. New York: Free Press.

Kohut, H. 1959. Introspection, empathy, and psychoanalysis. In *The Search for the Self*, 205–32. New York: International Universities Press, 1978.

———. 1968. The psychoanalytic treatment of narcissistic personality disorders. In *The Search for the Self*, 477–509. New York: International Universities Press, 1978.

———. 1971. *The Analysis of the Self*. New York: International Universities Press.

———. 1977. *The Restoration of the Self*. New York: International Universities Press.

———. 1978. *The Search for the Self*, ed. P. Ornstein. New York: International Universities Press.

———. 1984. *How Does Analysis Cure?* Ed. A. Goldberg and P. Stepansky. Chicago: University of Chicago Press.

Krystal, H. 1988. *Integration and Self-healing: Affect-Trauma-Alexithymia*. Hillsdale, NJ: Analytic Press.

Lacan, J. 1977. *Ecrits: A Selection*. New York: Norton.

Lassen, N. 1994. Where do people think? Presented at Psyche '94, Osaka, Japan, October.

Levenson, E. 1983. *The Ambiguity of Change*. New York: Basic Books.

Levin, F. 1991. *Mapping the Mind*. Hillsdale, NJ: Analytic Press.

———. 2003. *Psyche and Brain: The Biology of Talking Cures*. Madison, CT: International Universities Press.

———. 2004. Cytokines, psychoanalysis, and learning. In *Psychoanalysis in Dialogue with the Natural Sciences: Anglo-American Perspectives*, ed. P. Grampieri-Deutsch. Stuttgart: Kohlkammer Press.

Levin, F., and C. Trevarthen, C. 2000. Subtle is the Lord: The relationship between consciousness, the unconscious, and the executive control network (ECN) of the brain. *Annual of Psychoanalysis* 28:105–25.

Lichtenberg, J. 1983. *Psychoanalysis and Infant Research.* Hillsdale, NJ: Analytic Press.

———. 1989. *Psychoanalysis and Motivation.* Hillsdale, NJ: Analytic Press.

Lichtenstein, H. 1961. Identity and sexuality. *Journal of the American Psychoanalytic Association* 9:179–260.

Loewald, H. 1960. On the therapeutic action of psycho-analysis. *International Journal of Psycho-Analysis* 41:16–33.

———. 1989. *Sublimation.* New Haven, CT: Yale University Press.

Miller, J., M. Sabshin, J. Gedo, G. Pollock, L. Sadow, and N. Schlessinger. 1969. Some aspects of Charcot's influence on Freud. *Journal of the American Psychoanalytic Association* 17:608–23.

Mitchell, S. 1988. *Relational Concepts in Psychoanalysis: An Integration.* Cambridge, MA: Harvard University Press.

Modell, A. 1990. *Other Times, Other Realities.* Cambridge, MA: Harvard University Press.

———. 1992. The private self and private space. *Annual of Psychoanalysis* 20:1–14.

———. 1993. *The Private Self.* Cambridge, MA: Harvard University Press.

Moraitis, G. 1988. A reexamination of phobias as the fear of the unknown. *Annual of Psychoanalysis* 16:231–49.

Muller, J. 1996. *Beyond the Psychoanalytic Dyad.* New York: Routledge.

Muller, J. and W. Richardson. 1982. *Lacan and Language: A Reader's Guide to "Ecrits."* New York: International Universities Press.

Noy, P. 1969. A revision of the psychoanalytic theory of the primary process. *International Journal of Psycho-Analysis* 50:155–78.

Opatow, B. 1989. Drive theory and the metapsychology of experience. *International Journal of Psycho-Analysis* 70:645–60.

Palombo, S. 1978. *Dreaming and Memory: A New Information Processing Model.* New York: Basic Books.

Panksepp, J. 1998. *Affective Neuroscience: The Foundations of Human and Animal Emotions.* Oxford: Oxford University Press.

Rapaport, D. 1959. *The Structure of Psychoanalytic Theory: A Systematizing Attempt.* Psychological Issues, no. 6. New York: International Universities Press.

———. 1967. *The Collected Papers of David Rapaport,* ed. M. Gill. New York: Basic Books.

Rapaport, D., and M. Gill. 1959. The points of view and assumptions of metapsychology. *International Journal of Psycho-Analysis* 40:153–62.

Reich, O. 1933. *Character Analysis.* Reprint, New York: Orgone Institute Press, 1946.

Reiser, M. 1984. *Mind, Brain, Body: Toward a Convergence of Psychoanalysis and Neurobiology.* New York: Basic Books.

Robbins, M. 1987. Broadening the scope of psychoanalysis to include more seriously disturbed individuals. Presented to the Academy of Psychoanalysis, May, Chicago.

Rosenblatt, A., and J. Thickstun. 1977. *Modern Psychoanalytic Concepts in a General Psychology.* Psychological Issues, no. 42/43. New York: International Universities Press.

Rubinstein, B. 1965. Psychoanalytic theory and the mind-body problem. In *Psychoanalysis and Current Biological Thought,* ed. N. Greenfield and W. Lewis, 35–56. Madison: University of Wisconsin Press.

———. 1967. Explanation and mere description: A metascientific examination of certain aspects of the psychoanalytic theory of motivation. In *Psychology Versus Metapsychology*, ed. M. Gill and P. Holzman. Psychological Issues, no. 36, pp. 20–77. New York: International Universities Press.

———. 1974. On the role of classificatory processes in mental functioning: Aspects of a psychoanalytic theoretical model. *Psychoanalysis and Contemporary Science* 3:101–85.

———. 1976. On the possibility of a strictly clinical psychoanalytic theory: An essay in the philosophy of psychoanalysis. In *Psychology Versus Metapsychology*, ed. M. Gill and P. Holzman. Psychological Issues, no. 36, pp. 229–64. New York: International Universities Press, 1976.

———. 1997. *Psychoanalysis and the Philosophy of Science*, ed. R. Holt. Psychological Issues, no. 62/63. Madison, CT: International Universities Press.

Sadow, L., J. Gedo, J. Miller, G. Pollock, M. Sabshin, and N. Schlessinger. 1967. The process of hypothesis change in three early psychoanalytic concepts. *Journal of the American Psychoanalytic Association* 16:245–73.

Sadow, L., and A. Suslick. 1961. The simulation of a previous psychotic state. *Archives of General Psychiatry* 4:452–58.

Sander, L. 1980. Investigation of the infant and its caregiving environment as a biological system. In *The Course of Life*, vol. 1, ed. S. Greenspan and G. Pollock, 177–202. Rockville, MD: NIMH.

———. 1983. To begin with—reflections on ontogeny. In *Reflections on Self-Psychology*, ed. J. Lichtenberg and S. Kaplan, 85–104. Hillsdale, NJ: Analytic Press.

Schafer, R. 1970. An overview of Heinz Hartmann's contributions to psychoanalysis. In *A New Language for Psychoanalysis*. New Haven, CT: Yale University Press.

———. 1976. *A New Language for Psychoanalysis*. New Haven, CT: Yale University Press.

———. 1995. In the wake of Heinz Hartmann. *International Journal of Psycho-Analysis* 76:223–35.

Schore, A. 1994. *Affect Regulation and the Origin of the Self*. Hillsdale, NJ: Erlbaum.

Schwartz, A. 1987. Drives, affects, behavior—and learning: Approaches to a psychobiology of emotion and an integration of psychoanalytic and neurobiologic thought. *Journal of the American Psychoanalytic Association* 35:467–506.

Shane, E., and M. Shane. 1995. Living through: An aspect of the working through concept. *Journal of the American Psychoanalytic Association* 43:372–77.

Shevrin, H. 1997. Psychoanalysis as the patient: High in feeling, low in energy. *Journal of the American Psychoanalytic Association* 45:841–64.

Smith, H. 1997. Creative misreading. *Journal of the American Psychoanalytic Association* 45:335–57.

Spence, D. 1982. *Narrative Truth and Historical Truth*. New York: Norton.

Spitz, R. 1946. Anaclitic depression. *Psychoanalytic Study of the Child* 2:313–46.

Stepansky, P. 1983. *In Freud's Shadow: Adler in Context*. Hillsdale, NJ: Analytic Press.

Stern, D. 1985. *The Interpersonal World of the Infant*. New York: Basic Books.

Stoller, R. 1975. *Perversion: The Erotic Form of Hatred*. New York: Pantheon.

Stolorow, R., and G. Atwood. 1992. *Context of Being: The Intersubjective Foundations of Psychological Life*. Hillsdale, NJ: Analytic Press.

Sulloway, F. 1979. *Freud: Biologist of the Mind*. New York: Basic Books.

Summers, F. 1994. *Object Relations Theories and Psychopathology*. Hillsdale, NJ: Analytic Press.

Swanson, D. 1977. A critique of psychic energy as an explanatory concept. *Journal of the American Psychoanalytic Association* 25:603–33.

Tarachow, S. 1963. *An Introduction to Psychotherapy*. New York: International Universities Press.

Tomkins, S. 1962–1963. *Affect, Imagery, and Consciousness*. 2 vols. New York: Springer.

———. 1995. *Exploring Affect: The Selective Writings of Sylvan Tomkins*. Cambridge, UK: Cambridge University Press.

Toulmin, S. 1978. Psychoanalysis, physics, and the mind-body problem. *Annual of Psychoanalysis* 6:315–36.

Valenstein, A. 1973. On attachment to painful feelings and the negative therapeutic reaction. *Psychoanalytic Study of the Child* 28:365–92.

———. 1995. Working through in psychoanalysis: Discussion. *Journal of the American Psychoanalytic Association* 43:378–84.

Waelder, R. 1930. The principle of multiple function. In *Psychoanalysis, Observation, Theory, Application*, 68–83. New York: International Universities Press, 1976.

Wallerstein, R. 1986. *42 Lives in Treatment*. New York: Guilford.

Weiss, J., H. Sampson, and the Mt. Zion Psychotherapy Research Group. 1986. *The Psychoanalytic Process*. New York: Guilford.

Wilson, A., and J. Gedo, eds. 1993. *The Concept of Hierarchies in Psychoanalysis*. New York: Guilford.

Wilson, A., and Weinstein, L. 1992. An investigation into some implications for psychoanalysis of the Vygotskian view on the origins of mind. *Journal of the American Psychoanalytic Association* 40:357–87.

Winnicott, D. 1951. Transitional objects and transitional phenomena. In *Collected Papers*, 229–42. London: Tavistock, 1958.

———. 1954. Metapsychological and clinical aspects of regression within the psychoanalytic set-up. In *Collected Papers*, 278–94. London: Tavistock, 1958.

———. 1958. *Collected Papers*. London: Tavistock.

———. 1960. The theory of the parent-infant relationship. *International Journal of Psycho-Analysis* 41:585–95.

———. 1965. *The Maturational Processes and the Facilitating Environment*. New York: International Universities Press.

Wolf, E. 1976. Ambience and abstinence. *Annual of Psychoanalysis* 4:101–15.

———. 1992. On being a scientist or a healer: Reflections on abstinence, neutrality, and gratification. *Annual of Psychoanalysis* 20:115–30.

Wurmser, L. 1994. A time of questioning: The severely disturbed patient without classical psychoanalysis. *Annual of Psychoanalysis* 22:173–208.

Zetzel, E. 1965. The theory of therapy in relation to a developmental model of the psychic apparatus. *International Journal of Psycho-Analysis* 46:39–52.

Index

John E. Gedo practiced psychoanalysis for more than forty years. Formerly Training and Supervising Analyst at the Chicago Institute for Psychoanalysis and Clinical Professor of Psychiatry at the University of Illinois (Chicago), his most recent academic appointment was as Visiting Professor of Psychoanalytic Thought at the University of Chicago.

Gedo has published extensively on the theory and the intellectual history of psychoanalysis, including *The Languages of Psychoanalysis* (1996) and *The Evolution of Psychoanalysis* (1999). *Psychoanalysis as Biological Science* is his twentieth book.